PROFIT BUILDING

PROFIT BUILDING
Cutting Costs Without Cutting People

Perry J. Ludy

Berrett-Koehler Publishers, Inc.
San Francisco

Berrett-Koehler Publishers, Inc.
450 Sansome Street, Suite 1200
San Francisco, CA 94111-3320
Tel: (415) 288-0260
Fax: (415) 362-2512
www.bkconnection.com

ORDERING INFORMATION
Quantity sales. Special discounts are available on quantity purchases by corporations, associations, and others. For details, contact the "Special Sales Department" at the Berrett-Koehler address above.

Individual sales. Berrett-Koehler publications are available through most bookstores. They can also be ordered direct from Berrett-Koehler: Tel: (800) 929-2929; Fax: (802) 864-7626; www.bkconnection.com

Orders for college textbook/course adoption use. Please contact Berrett-Koehler: Tel: (800) 929-2929; Fax: (802) 864-7626.

Orders by U.S. trade bookstores and wholesalers. Please contact Publishers Group West, 1700 Fourth Street, Berkeley, CA 94710. Tel: (510) 528-1444; Fax (510) 528-3444.

Printed in the United States of America
Printed on acid-free and recycled paper that is composed of 85% recovered fiber, including 15% post consumer waste.

Library of Congress Cataloging-in-Publication Data

Ludy, Perry J.
    Profit building : cutting costs without cutting people / by Perry J. Ludy.
      p. cm.
    Includes bibliographical references and index.
    ISBN 1-57675-108-2 (alk. paper)
    1. Cost control. 2. Profit. 3. Teams in the workplace. 4. Industrial management. I. Title.

HD47.3 L83 2000
658.15'52—dc21
                                            00-031162

First Edition
05   04   03   02   01   00   10 9 8 7 6 5 4 3 2 1

To my wife, Lynda, who played a major role in the development of this book.

Contents

Preface

Improving profits is one of the main objectives of business, yet based on my 25 years of experience as a senior executive with direct profit and loss accountability, I have observed that most managers do not truly understand how to move beyond the basics of cost reduction and profit improvement.

Rapid changes in technology and the world market exacerbate this problem, making profit improvement harder to achieve than ever before. Increasingly, organizations across the country and throughout the world face the difficult tasks of developing and then executing an e-strategy, meeting the challenge of globalization, and keeping up with fierce competition. Innovation and change have become the centerpiece of our business environment. Business leaders, entrepreneurs, small business owners, and managers are struggling to find the tools they need to achieve success and avoid the pitfalls of inappropriate strategies. Yet it is interesting to note that even though the business environment is changing and the challenges are becoming more difficult, profit improvement continues to be a key part of the solution.

Could there be a more effective way to focus our daily business activities? If profit improvement is one of the essential elements of our business strategies and challenges, why don't we develop the ability to focus continuously on profit improvement the same way we focus on marketing, operations, and human resources? Why don't cost reduction and the resources and leadership necessary for its success receive management's constant attention? *Profit Building* answers these questions. It demonstrates how a large corporation, a small business, or a single department can improve profits and reduce costs, using a proven approach that is based on *team* innovation management.

This book is a blueprint for executives, managers, business professionals, small business owners, and change leaders who are seeking appropriate profit improvement strategies for their organizations. It shows how companies can benefit—rather than suffer—from the unprecedented changes occurring in today's marketplace. It also makes the point that in order to achieve success beyond today, business leaders must leverage the total means available within the organization to improve profits, reduce costs, and create a better place to work.

Typically, a company's knee-jerk response to the need to reduce costs is to reduce the workforce. People are laid off in large numbers, and dollars are saved—or so it seems. In most situations this is a mistake or merely a short-term solution. The better approach is to give employees a chance to participate in developing cost reduction strategies so that profit improvement is perpetual. In this scenario, people are not laid off in large numbers but, instead, are better utilized within the organization. This is the approach that I have found the most successful, and it is the basis of this book.

Profit Building introduces the methodology of the Profit Building Process (PBP): a system of step-by-step activities designed to produce immediate and ongoing results. PBP shows managers how to apply concepts gleaned from prior learning to create appropriate strategies for many different types of organizations and businesses.

Why I Wrote This Book

I have always wanted a book about how to increase profits. Yet each time I searched for such a book, I was forced to settle for a publication on business theory, financial management, or process costing. Throughout my career, I never found a book that specifically told me how to take a business, organization, department, or team through an easy-to-follow process to achieve cost reduction or profit improvement. No matter what our industry or management position, we all need creative new ideas on how to make our business more profitable. This book is designed to meet these needs.

Profit Building is an easy-to-read road map to profit improvement. It explains a simple process by which business leaders can stimulate employees' thinking and problem-solving skills, thereby generating a multitude of creative ideas and effective solutions for profit improvement. This book also includes a list of more than 100 innovative ideas generated through the PBP approach that can be applied to most businesses with immediate results.

I wanted to develop a valuable handbook for executives and managers who do not have time to read volumes on business theory, and I believe that this brief book offers an effective short cut. *Profit Building* embraces most managers' knowledge of familiar business concepts, moving beyond abstract theory to actual demonstrations of how to get quickly to the point of reducing costs and boosting profits. This book introduces the basic concepts of the Profit Building Process, showing managers both how to get started and how to move on to a higher level of performance.

Who Should Read This Book

Because profit improvement and cost reduction should be every manager's responsibility, I believe that this book is most effective when all managers in the organization read it. Anyone concerned with improving profits will find it useful. If every manager and every supervisor follow the techniques discussed here, eventually the whole company will be contributing to the process of profit building. Senior executives, consultants, small business owners, and accountants will find this book valuable. Of course, profit improvement is a worldwide business objective, and international business leaders will also find some cost-cutting tactics of interest. The bottom line is that *everyone builds profit.*

As you read this book, you will find that PBP uses a team approach to achieving profitability. Managers should make *Profit Building* a part of their training programs, and all employees should become aware of the opportunities for cost reduction that surround them and should actively participate in perpetual profit improvement. Ideally, Profit Building is a company-wide program spearheaded by a profit building team.

I have enjoyed writing this book and am confident that reading it will be beneficial to all those who seek a direct, proven method for profit improvement in a simple, informative format. My hope is that through this book, more companies will realize that profit improvement is an ongoing process that demands constant attention and company-wide participation. Many cost reduction questions can be answered by those who know the situation best—the employees. Please read on to discover how to develop this forgotten "people-resource" in the search for profit improvement.

1 What Managers Need to Know About Cutting Costs and Improving Profits

Ah, to build, to build!
That is the noblest art of all the arts.
—HENRY WADSWORTH LONGFELLOW

In our businesses, we are continually challenged to reshape our organizations in order to utilize and preserve the resources that fuel profitability. We have put organizations in place, and continue to operate them, in accordance with the philosophy that control, compliance, structure, procedures, and policies lead to a profitable organization. Most of today's business books emphasize similar organizational structure and departments (marketing, human resources, finance, and so on). Remarkably, however, there is one key area where we continue to miss the mark. We do not view profit generation as an organizational function, and as a result, it is not managed as a process. Organizations need to view profit building as a process similar to the processes that drive marketing, human resources, and finance. Wouldn't it be refreshing if, on your next business trip, the person seated next to you introduced herself as the director of profit building for XYZ Corporation. I believe most investors would attempt to purchase stock in that company as soon as they could! This book introduces the Profit Building Process (PBP), an innovative concept based on incorporating profit improvement teams into the daily processes of the organization or business.

When viewed as a process, profit building can be broken down into a series of straightforward procedures that are in many ways similar to the process of constructing a building. Using the Profit Building Process as our blueprint, we begin with a strong foundation—in this case, a *well-trained and well-prepared team.* The next step is to construct a framework by *asking all the pertinent questions,* just as a plumber, electrician, or carpenter might do before undertaking a task. In the case of building profits, this amounts to *brainstorming for appropriate solutions.* Then construction begins. Profit building is in progress and *action steps* are implemented. Finally, in both examples a *review and follow-up* must be implemented to ensure that everything is "to code."

Regrettably, many companies have no plan at all for profit building. Thus it is not surprising that when profits sag, these companies cut costs the only way they know how. They strip the organization of the most significant resource it has: people.

This response to reducing costs is all too common. We live in a world where mergers, acquisitions, and leveraged buyouts have become the norm. Profitable organizations are being acquired by investor groups that gain tremendously by downsizing, reducing large numbers of employees, and focusing on short-term returns. When they deliver short-term results, senior executives are rewarded with stock options that build wealth. Increasing shareholder value is the "shield" behind which investor groups and boards of directors hide as they sell cash flow and other assets—and garner rich rewards. Yet these once-solid, profitable organizations now have considerably more debt, and management has a chance to reap additional rewards by finding new ways to service this debt—usually, by enforcing further layoffs.

This book can help reverse that trend. A blueprint for success, *Profit Building* shows how organizations that are sensitive to team dynamics can take advantage of a broad range of opportunities to improve profitability continuously, and achieve cost reduction, *without layoffs.* As organizations increasingly find themselves evaluating and planning the near-term and long-term future of the business, managers must delve into and make use of all the means available within the organization to reduce cost on an ongoing basis and consistently improve profits. This includes developing the people who make up the teams that support the business. In other words, business leaders must learn how to mine the organization not only for hidden profits but also for hidden *people-*resources. Whether you are an international business leader, corporate executive, manager, business professional, entrepreneur, or change leader, this book will help you effectively develop teams dedicated to profit improvement. But before we delve into the details of the Profit Building Process, let's examine how profit improvement is currently addressed in *your* organization.

■ The Profit Improvement Paradox

In most business conversations, only moments pass before some reference is made to improving profits. This is predictable because a main focus of business is to make profits. What is not so predictable is most managers' limited ability to formulate effective plans for profit improvement. This is what I refer to as the Profit Improvement Paradox: Although a key goal of management is to improve profitability and reduce costs, few managers have the tools or ability to do so. How can that be? It is profit that drives the Wall Street machine. It is profit that drives shareholder interest. It is profit that drives return on investment. Our managers should be profit pros, but few are. Although this paradox pervades today's business environment, it is so deeply entrenched and so well camouflaged that I fear business leaders will continue to overlook it. If profit improvement is a main goal of business, why is it that most business people do not know how to reduce costs continuously?

Let's take a few moments to test for the existence of the Profit Improvement Paradox in *your* company. Conduct the following exercise with a cross section of your management team.

The Profit Improvement Paradox Test

A. Choose a group of 10 to 15 managers from different areas of responsibility within your organization, including human resources, finance, marketing, operations, training, information technology, purchasing, engineering, and telecommunications. Their experience level can range from junior managers to senior executives. If you are a small business owner or department head of a large corporation, choose diverse members from your company or team.

B. Call an impromptu meeting, asking your managers to come to a conference room with a blank pad of paper and a pen. It is important that you not inform them of the nature of the meeting in advance.

C. Once they are assembled, have them quickly write down, to the best of their ability, their answers to the following questions.

1. What are the top five most costly items on your profit and loss statement?

2. What written action plans are in place to reduce cost for those five line items?

3. What are your variable costs and what have you done to reduce them?

4. What are your fixed costs and what have you done to reduce them?

5. Name five vendors from whom you purchase supplies or services. When was the last time you negotiated a better price from these vendors?

6. Which of your costs are down from a year ago and why?

7. What have you done to reduce labor costs in your area of responsibility?

8. What are you doing this week to reduce costs on your next P&L statement?

9. How do you know you are being charged the correct rate on your long-distance telephone bills?

10. What amount of cost reduction is planned for next month?

D. When they have finished, ask your managers to read their answers aloud. Take time to discuss each response as a group. During this process, notice your managers' reactions: Are there blank looks? Do few leaders emerge? Do their answers lack innovative, proactive approaches? Are there few written action steps?

E. Now ask your managers what *they* believe are the main objectives of business, and write their responses on a flip chart. Most should agree that profit improvement and cost reduction are main objectives. (If not, you have some work to do!) Then discuss the paradox: If profit improvement and cost reduction are main objectives, why is it that so few managers were prepared to answer the questions you asked? What do they focus on each day? Where does their time go? Clearly, it is time to reprioritize.

I believe most of us would agree that the questions in this exercise are pretty basic. After all, profitability is a main objective of business, right? Yet your managers' responses are not unusual. As I mentioned, the Profit Improvement Paradox is insidious, and one that many of your managers may be shocked to discover.

■ Development of the Profit Building Process

The Profit Building Process (PBP) is a step-by-step method for developing people-resources, analyzing the situation, and coming up with creative solutions. Built around the team concept, PBP relies on the creative thinking of a diverse team of managers and employees who represent various departments in the company. Training in innovation management, a unique brainstorming method, and developing action plans are the backbone of the PBP process. An organized system of follow-up and accountability, along with continuous input from managers and employees, ensures PBP's success.

PBP is not a fad—it is a set of sound, reliable business practices with a humanistic bent. For the past 25 years, I have seen it used in a variety of industries in corporations across the United States and internationally, including manufacturing, retail, restaurants, banking, and automotive testing. It works for small businesses and multi-million-dollar corporations alike. The process grew out of my background in human resources and my experience in senior operations positions.

My business career began in 1974 at Procter & Gamble. Fresh out of college, I was hired into the company's training program for entry-level management. There I gained an understanding of the importance of two principles that have become the foundation of PBP:

1. *Team Preparation.* Through regularly scheduled team meetings (usually a half-hour at the start of each day), the team sharpens its skills with team-building and problem-solving exercises. This way, when a real problem arises, the team has the tools and ability to find the best solutions.
2. *Employee Participation.* The workforce must be involved in the problem-solving situations that constantly arise. In other words, most problems should be addressed at the lowest possible level of the organization through managed team participation.

I further developed this people-based approach while working for PepsiCo as a human resources professional. I was approached by a president of one of its divisions about participating in PepsiCo's senior management designate program, a fast-track strategy to develop future leaders of the organization. During my participation in this 24-month skills development program, I was trained to become a vice president with general management responsibilities for 20,000 employees and $500 million in revenue. Keep in mind that before I entered this program, my background was in human resources with a focus on developing people, team building, and training. Once I completed the program, I became a general manager with responsibility for net operating profits after taxes and for return on assets employed. Because of my human resources background, my approach to solving marketing and finance problems was rooted in the development of people and team consulting. Now, after 25 years of trial and error, I have devised and refined a program for cost reduction and profit improvement that can be applied with immediate results to any business situation. The Profit Building Process always mines the background and experience of the people driving innovation in the organization. In addition, PBP includes important strategies and insights on how to prepare the company for coming change—a process imperative to successful implementation.

The act of *preparing* the organization for change is a step that is often overlooked. Time and time again we have seen innovative ideas, which appear to have merit and seem to be just what the business needs, turn "dead on arrival" because the business is just not ready for them. Furthermore, many organizations are never aware that such a problem exists; managers assume that the *idea* must be faulty, never recognizing that the real fault lies in the organization's inability to accept change. *Profit Building* addresses this dilemma by providing some basic guidance on how to prepare both the profit building team and the organization to recognize barriers to change. The book also offers a variety of solutions that will help increase the rate at which new ideas are successfully adopted.

So why rely on layoffs? This book offers innovative alternatives to workforce reduction and makes the most of employees' desire to participate in enhancing profits. It shows organizations how to give employees that opportunity through a process that perpetuates cost reduction and helps sustain profit improvement. In fact, throughout this book you will discover a wide variety of new concepts and methods for cost reduction and profit improvement, including

1. The Organizational Complexity Predictor, a 20-question survey that measures an organization's ability to accept change.

2. Questions Brainstorming, wherein participants explore a topic by brainstorming an endless list of questions, rather than trying to come up with immediate answers. These questions are then carefully dissected, and the answers become the starting point for new profit improvement programs.

3. Preparing the organization for a renewed focus on profit improvement, just as you would prepare the organization for a renewed focus on quality or for reengineering.

4. Adopting the practice of holding regular meetings on profit improvement, thereby getting the organization into the habit of "ritualizing" profit improvement.

5. Not going after all profits at once, but instead focusing on one initiative at a time, and then re-igniting the profit building process to launch a new initiative once the previous action item has been completed.

6. A list of more than 100 cost reduction and profit improvement ideas for generating immediate results.

This is a book about profit improvement and cost reduction! It is designed to help business managers benefit, rather than suffer, from unprecedented organizational transitions. Conscientiously applied, PBP will produce long-term results for any organization or business.

2 | Improving Profits: Better Ways Than Layoffs

> *Business must be profitable if it is to continue to succeed, but the glory of business is to make it so successful that it may do things that are great chiefly because they ought to be done.*
> —CHARLES SCHWAB

One of the first times I witnessed the power of a team in action was in 1975, when I was a manager at Procter & Gamble. It was approximately two years after the Charmin paper plant in Oxnard, California had opened, and sales had failed to meet our projections. It was a typical scenario: All managers were called into a meeting and told about the shortfall in revenue. Because sales had slipped, we were instructed to come up with a plan to cut costs by 10% in each of our departments.

I was among 20 managers in this meeting. Each of us had a team of employees who had been hired over the last year. When we reconvened to present our plans, 19 out of 20 of us proposed to cut costs through layoffs. Thanks to my team, my plan was different.

When I had taken the problem to my team to solve, the scope and variety of their answers had amazed me. Through brainstorming and teamwork, we had developed an action plan that significantly cut costs without cutting jobs. The plan we came up with included the following recommendations:

- *All employees would take an across-the-board pay cut during this period of revenue shortfall, as long as there would be an opportunity to earn back missed wages via incentives in future months.*

- *The team would organize a process for volunteers to take personal time off.*

- *We would use smaller containers for packaging product.*

- *We would reschedule the railroad cars, change truck shipping methods that utilized less than a full load, and combine customer shipping to make routes more cost-efficient.*

- *We would develop a procedure to change the way product was received from other departments to reduce damage and save time.*

- *We would review a recommendation to redesign the warehouse to improve efficiency in shipping and receiving.*

- *We would review a recommendation to streamline the way customers' orders were taken.*

Thanks to our plan, we did not have to lay off key people in the organization who had been hired and trained just a year before. We were able to save jobs while still cutting costs. And, as is usually the case, sales volume reversed its downward trend. Had we resorted to layoffs, we would have had to rehire these valuable people—if they were still available.

My team appreciated the opportunity to be involved in the problem-solving process. It gave them some control over the fate of their jobs, as well as a chance to contribute to the operation of the organization on a larger scale.

As I look back on that situation at Procter & Gamble, I realize that it was a significant milestone in my transition to senior management. I learned something that has remained a part of my management style throughout my career. You don't need to eliminate people to effect a short-term return. Get your people involved in the problem-solving process, and you will quickly find appropriate and lasting solutions.

■ The Downsizing Dilemma

Unfortunately, many companies did not learn this lesson. Throughout the 1980s and 1990s, downsizing was embraced as a quick and easy way to keep costs under control. Most such companies are now discovering the long-term disadvantages of having grabbed these short-term gains.

Reeling from the effects of downsizing, organizations are scrambling for ways to keep pace in today's active marketplace, with their smaller, less experienced staffs. Industry magazines are full of advice on how to pick up the pieces after downsizing has taken its toll. *Internet Telephony* characterized the effect of downsizing in the telephone industry this way:

> It is clear that the downsizing strategy generally used to prepare for competition is beginning to exhaust its usefulness. Just when salespeople need to be most enthusiastic about battling for and keeping customers, they're feeling the effects of downsizing.
>
> As the *Wall Street Journal* pointed out last summer, "After a decade of frantic cost cutting, the downside of downsizing is beginning to take its toll: Decimated sales staffs turn in lousy numbers. 'Survivor syndrome' takes hold, and over-burdened staffers just go through the motions of working."[1]

Many other companies have discovered the downside of downsizing. In 1995, Connecticut Mutual Life Insurance Company tried to reduce costs by reducing its workforce. Its strategy was to offer a lucrative buyout program to its 1675 employees. About 900 workers—twice as many as expected—accepted the offer, forcing the company to refill 400 positions. Consequently, Connecticut Mutual Life ended up paying out an estimated $16.9 million in severance pay to eliminate jobs it later refilled.[2]

Eastman Kodak made similar blunders. To make up for the loss of employees after layoffs, the company began outsourcing work at peak periods. In many instances, the contractors charged 3 to 4 times more than the company had paid their former employees to perform the same work. Kodak eventually restaffed some of the positions it eliminated.[3]

At Nynex Corporation, layoffs resulted in poor customer service and heavy penalties. In 1996, the company was ordered by New York's Public Service Commission to rebate $50 million to customers because its reduced staff fell behind in responding to problems and requests. Eventually, Nynex ended up rehiring hundreds of former employees, many of them managers who were already receiving company pensions.[4]

Professor Nitin Nohria of the Harvard Business School has studied the effects of downsizing on America's top 100 companies. According to Professor Nohria, although downsizing yields short-term shareholder gains, it hampers economic growth and undermines long-term competitiveness. With few exceptions, the companies he studied had all downsized repeatedly, cutting their workforce an average of 20%. However, most had not seen improved results. Nohria comments:

> It's not that layoffs are good or bad, but that there are good layoffs and bad layoffs. There seem to be two approaches to downsizing. The first type, which we found among two-thirds of the companies we studied, was a simple, across-the-board cost-cutting approach. Most of those downsizings failed to produce productivity gains or profits over a three-year period subsequent to the layoffs.
>
> The second type, practiced by the other third of the companies we looked at, was more discriminating, motivated by a strategic vision of how to regain competitiveness. On average those firms improved their performances in the medium term.

After a decade of downsizing, organizations throughout the United States and around the world are experiencing the repercussions and are focusing on finding better ways to become more profitable. The challenges that these organizations now face include e-business, e-commerce, new competitors, globalization, technological advances, and the high cost of doing business. In reaction to these new challenges, some organizations still resort to downsizing, reorganizing, and (in some cases) ineffective production changes. Unfortunately, such actions produce only short-term results for many of these businesses. I believe many of these organizations have the resources to provide the funds they need, if only business owners and managers knew where to look.

As a senior executive with experience in five different industries, I was often hired to help floundering businesses to survive and healthy businesses to improve. In most cases, the money they were seeking was right under their noses. Yet countless times I saw top managers flailing about for solutions. They knew instinctively that the solutions were there, but they just could not find them, like someone searching for a light switch in the dark. This dilemma commonly affects managers who are not properly focused on profit improvement and cost reduction strategies. Few people would argue that improvement in profitability and reduction of costs are the most critical aspects of business today. But instead of focusing on these vital areas, most managers rely on traditional short-term solutions that often turn out to be critical mistakes for the organization. The two most common mistakes that we as business leaders continue to make in search of increased profits are as follows:

1. We continue to lay off large numbers of people who are the key resources essential to improving profitability.
2. We do not effectively train management to improve profits.

According to the American Psychological Association, workers who have been laid off feel betrayed and are less likely to feel loyalty toward future employers. "At the heart of these layoffs is the severing of the 'psychological contract' that has traditionally bound professionals to their employers," said Steve Kozlowski, Ph.D., in an article on downsizing published in the *APA Monitor*. According to Kozlowski,

> Before the 1990s, it was generally understood that employers would train professional workers and not lay them off willy-nilly; in return, the employees would work hard and not take their skills elsewhere. Suddenly you have to change that. And you lose loyalty when the rules change.[5]

Demographically, laid-off workers are a cross section of all of us who make up the business population: Some have families, some have college degrees, and some have 5, 10, or 15 years of experience and have helped to build the organization to its current level. Some have turned down other opportunities during their careers and thus have remained loyal to the organization, trusting it to continue providing them with gainful employment. In many cases, these individuals are at the most productive stage of their work lives and can contribute much more than ever before because of their knowledge, motivation, and relevant experience—not to mention the "chemistry" that develops when a team has performed together over the years.

Eliminating these people from our payrolls is our first mistake, and we repeat it time and time again. These people have the answers to the profit improvement questions—if management would just ask. Having experienced people participate in the cost reduction process generates long-term solutions that stabilize transitions and deliver levels of improvement many times greater than those generated by a massive one-time layoff.

Our second mistake is that management is not prepared to deliver improved profits. Most managers do not know how to reduce costs or improve profits, even though profitability improvement is on the mind of all managers.

I do not deny that there are situations wherein a company may have no alternative but to reduce the workforce to reduce costs, but I feel this method of cost reduction should always be considered a last resort. Unfortunately, many companies rely on layoffs for cost reduction, and other alternatives are never explored. So often, however, a little creative thinking and ingenuity can save jobs, while achieving the cost reduction goal.

■ Perpetuating the Profit Improvement Paradox

Although improving profits and reducing costs are a main objective of business, few managers have the tools or ability to achieve these goals. Before we can dispel the profit improvement paradox, we need to examine why this paradox exists. I believe there are four basic reasons: management distraction, a lack of management training, high management turnover, and the lack of a consistent process for focusing on profitability improvement. Let's take a closer look.

Management Distraction

Instead of focusing on profitability and cost reduction, most managers become distracted by other aspects of their business. The factors that contribute to this distraction include new competition, e-strategy opportunities, the need to improve efficiency, market share strategies, new technology, procedural changes, reengineering, and, yes, even serving the customer.

Clearly, these are vital areas that routinely demand immediate and constant attention. No one can deny their value to successful business operations. Even so, companies should have an ongoing cost reduction process running in the background of such critical activities, allowing profit improvement to continue. If management could only refocus on profitability, then it would generate long-term positive results that would become the catalyst for ongoing profit improvement. It is this continuous focus on cost reduction and profit increase that is the basis of *Profit Building*.

Lack of Management Training

There is a growing trend among companies today to increase their spending on management training. This is extremely important. However, these dollars need to be redeployed to support current initiatives. As organizations continue to prepare their managers to meet the challenges posed by today's business environment, they must also earmark adequate dollars for training managers to become more aware of profit improvement scenarios. Such training should be increased proportionately in order to equalize or offset the distractions that will always tend to undermine the profit improvement process.

Unfortunately, many companies still refuse to recognize the importance of training programs, and those that are willing to spend the money are not sure what type of training is needed. Upon evaluation of how much money is allocated to training associated with profit improvement or cost reduction it becomes very clear that in many companies, this type of training does not exist.

If your organization is one of the few that provides training specifically designed for profit improvement, ask yourself, "Does my training program offer a process for continued focus on cost reduction and the generation of innovative ideas to reduce future costs?" If the answer is yes, then I congratulate you! If the answer is "no," read on.

Management Turnover

Management turnover is a problem that most businesses must deal with on a regular basis. Its impact on your business is twofold: You lose the experience, knowledge, and training invested in the manager who leaves, and each replacement takes you back to zero in terms of cost reduction and any associated activities that have taken place.

Cost reduction and profitability improvement should stand alone as a constant, dynamic process that is not affected by management turnover. This process should become a core competency of the business. Therefore, profit improvement training should be a part of every new manager's development program.

Lack of a Consistent Process for Profit Improvement

I see this as the main reason why the profitability paradox exists. Too many organizations simply do not have a consistent, systematic process for reducing costs and improving profits on a continuous basis. That is why it is so difficult for managers, business owners, and even senior executives to identify quickly any action steps taken toward cost reduction. They tend to be more comfortable with problem solving when the questions require broad-based solutions that may or may not tie into profit improvement. When asked, for example, "What thoughts do you have regarding efficiency improvement and its impact on profitability?" or "How will our reengineering activity generate higher levels of profitability?" managers may respond with answers or solutions that cover a wide spectrum of possibilities.

Conversely, when asked more specifically, "What line items on the P&L statement do your areas of responsibility cover, and what steps are you taking to reduce those costs?" managers become more halting in their answers.

Many books that have been written about cost management focus on activity-based practices. Most widely known is Activity-Based Costing, or ABC, which is addressed in such titles as *Activity Accounting: An Activity-Based Costing Approach,* by James Brimson. There are also books on activity-based budgeting and activity-based management. These excellent books offer a great deal of information about cost measurement. Once you have read them, however, you may find yourself asking, "But how do I *reduce* my costs after I have measured them carefully?" and "Where can I find a list of cost reduction *ideas* organized by line item?" The answers to these questions are the basis for this book. Without them, continuous improvements in profitability are unlikely.

■ Summary

In most instances, the massive layoffs of the last decade have proved to be costly and ineffective. Yet many managers are unable to come up with alternative cost-cutting solutions. Business leaders make two common mistakes in the search for profit improvement:

1. They continue to lay off large numbers of people who are the key resources essential for profit improvement.

2. They do not effectively train managers to improve profits.

The profit improvement paradox is perpetuated by the attitudes and actions of management. The four main reasons for this are management distraction, lack of management training, management turnover, and lack of a consistent process for profit improvement.

The Profit Building Process can turn this trend around. The next chapter introduces the five steps of PBP and explains how to generate a multitude of cost reduction and profit improvement ideas—so that layoffs will always be used as a last resort.

3 | The Profit Building Process

> *True creativity is characterized by a succession of acts*
> *each dependent on the one before and suggesting the*
> *one after.*
> —EDWIN H. LAND, Inventor and founder of the
> Polaroid Corporation

W*hile I was president of a national auto glass company,*
we were faced with what must be an ongoing battle within many
organizations that have a widespread sales force: how to reduce sales
force costs while continuing to address customer needs, establish
customer relationships, and develop new prospects. My initial ap-
proach seemed logical but ended in disaster. I pulled a report on the
past three years of revenue generation and associated expenses. I
then chose a cross section of the sales force and asked them to meet
with their supervisor and me. Can you imagine inviting 11 sales
professionals to a meeting to discuss why they should reduce their
costs? In their view, their budgets were already too tight. After the
first hour, I had to end the meeting for fear that they would con-
vince me to authorize increasing the level of spending to hold on to
the customers we had! I quickly realized that there was no way I
was going to obtain compliance without demoralizing them. I had
to take a different approach.

I tried a method that had worked well for me in other organizations.
We put together a cross-functional team representing human re-
sources, finance, information technology, operations, and two mem-

bers of the sales staff. I have found that the differing viewpoints of a cross-functional team are often the catalyst for a breakthrough idea. Their broad knowledge base and diverse experiences usually result in a wider range of creative solutions. A team of people drawn from the same department or from similar positions often takes a narrow view, seeing only one or two solutions. In fact, I have observed cases where such a team could not imagine any alternative other than the one it represented.

Our cross-functional team was highly successful. Using the methods outlined in Profit Building, we brainstormed the following question: "Are there ways for the sales force to continue to call on the same number of customers and make the same number of prospecting calls at a reduced level of expense?" Of course, the answer to this question is "yes," and this team came up with a long list of ideas and suggestions ranging from technology improvement to reorganization of the sales force.

What went right? The team dynamics stand out. When peers from various departments were introduced into the process, a different type of communication took place. The sales representatives were more agreeable to peer suggestions. The atmosphere was more conducive to change. It was an entirely different meeting from the one I had previously held with the sales team. I witnessed firsthand the power of a cross-functional team.

One of the ideas generated was so innovative that it warrants special mention. The team looked at the last three years' costs to determine the average cost of

    A. *A night in a hotel*
    B. *An airplane trip*
    C. *A rental car*
    D. *A business meal*
    E. *A personal meal*

We then reexamined the list to determine which costs the sales representatives could best control. The team decided that they could help control the costs of all except the airplane trip. Then came the idea that really got the sales representatives' attention: Why not give incentives to sales representatives whose costs are less than the average rates?

Example:

> *The average night's stay at a hotel was $139.00. The company wanted to reduce that expense by 20%. Therefore, our target was to spend $113.00 per night.*

> *The team recommended that the travel policy be changed to state that the company would reimburse every night's hotel stay at $113.00, no matter what the actual cost. If sales representatives stayed at hotels that cost less than $113.00, they would be allowed to "pocket the difference," thus earning compensation for their thrift at no extra cost to the company.*

> *This same concept was applied to rental cars, business meals, and personal meals. With the help of the new incentive, the sales staff found ways to reduce the same costs that a few weeks earlier had been thought impossible to lower. The results got my attention. We were able to reduce the line items associated with hotel cost, rental car cost, personal meals, and entertainment by 20% without cutting people! This would not have happened but for the cross-functional team approach. This approach is so effective that it is the basis of the Profit Building Process.*

■ Just What Is PBP?

Simply put, PBP is a five-step process for cost reduction and profit improvement. Through this process, an established team, trained in innovation management and "Questions Brainstorming," develops the necessary action steps for a performance improvement plan. Review and follow-up then direct the process back to the team for a new cycle of creativity.

Thus PBP acts as an engine for continuous improvement, produces immediate results, and becomes a core competency.

PBP consists of the following five steps:

1. Picking Your Team
2. Preparing Your Team and the Organization
3. Brainstorming All the Questions
4. Taking Action and Documenting Results
5. Reviewing and Following Up

Each step plays a vital role in the process. Systematically applied, they generate a synergistic approach that delivers constant, continuous focus and improvement. *Profit Building* assumes that readers have a basic understanding of the general business concepts discussed in this book. The principal focus of the book is the systematic application of these concepts to reduce costs and improve profits.

A brief description of each of the five steps follows. Then, in Chapters 4–8, each step is discussed in a manner that fully illustrates its critical role in the PBP process.

Step 1. Picking Your Team

The first step is to pick a team. The team is the foundation of the PBP process; it is the platform for voicing opinions, the means for gathering information, and the tool for analyzing cost reduction and profit improvement. Your team's primary purpose is finding innovative solutions or ideas to reduce cost within every line of the profit and loss statement. Therefore, your team members should be innovative thinkers with a wide range of experiences to draw on. Because the team concept is a popular topic—there are dozens of books on the subject—managers generally have a good understanding of the importance of teams and how to apply some of the basic principles of team building. For this reason, Chapter 4 focuses on team building as it applies specifically to the Profit Building Team (PBT). If you would like more information on teams, I recommend *The Wisdom of Teams: Creating the High-Performance Organization* by Jon R. Katzenback and Douglas K. Smith (New York: HarperBusiness, 1994) and *The Art of Facilitation:*

How to Create Group Synergy, by Dale Hunter (New York: Fisher Books, 1995).

The basic principles that guide the building of the PBT team are (1) the size of the team, (2) the need for diverse skills, (3) the team's purpose, (4) the team's goals, and (5) team responsibilities.

Step 2: Preparing Your Team and the Organization

In Step 2 of the PBP approach, each team member must be "prepared" to understand the techniques of innovation management. Chapter 5 explains the fundamental steps that prepare team members to recognize the enablers of innovations as well as how to deal with the setbacks that occur as the innovation process unfolds. The process also takes into account certain factors—such as the size of the organization, its age, and the number of times an idea has been tried—and how these factors will affect the success or failure of the idea.

As part of my discussions of this step, I have included a training program that should be used to help prepare the team for these enablers of innovation. I must stress the importance of completing this training. Preparing the team through innovation training is the key to implementing the ideas the team comes up with in the brainstorming process. During training, the team will learn to recognize and measure a company's ability to change, to lay the groundwork for future innovations, to measure an idea's success, and to make needed adjustments. This process also teaches the team how to turn to the workforce for answers to tough questions—and thus tap input that can make the difference between success and failure. Do not skip this training! Also included is a list of ideas on how to prepare the organization for change.

Step 3. Brainstorming All the Questions

Once the team is chosen and its members are prepared for innovation management, the next step is to take the team through a facilitated brainstorming exercise, with a twist. Chapter 6 introduces "Questions Brainstorming" and demonstrates how to brainstorm the questions that generate answers, ideas, solutions, action steps, and so on. Brainstorming questions instead of answers stimulates teams to be more creative when exploring a topic. The challenge of coming up with question after question takes teams through a thinking process that ultimately leads to the development of appropriate answers, and these then become the action items for the performance improvement planning process that follows. This critical step will prove far more successful than traditional brainstorming methods, which often result in shallow and temporary answers or solutions.

A key benefit of asking questions is that managers are able to brainstorm questions until they are satisfied that they have a true understanding of the objectives and solutions, rather than attempting to generate quick answers in areas where they may be inexperienced. This process also encourages total team participation, because most members find it easy to come up with a list of questions. The ease of the process facilitates creative thinking, leading to better questions and (ultimately) better solutions. For example, when a team is brainstorming the high cost of a line item on the P&L, the Questions Brainstorming process might go like this:

- What is the chart of accounts that make up this line item?
- Why do we have this cost?
- Are there other alternatives?
- Are there other ways to handle this item?
- Are we charged the proper amount?
- What is the price for this service?
- When did we last negotiate this item?

Continue asking questions until you feel you have exhausted the topic. Only when *all* the questions have been asked is it time to start looking for answers. Each team member should be assigned the task of finding the answers to specific questions on your list. (You may need to prioritize the questions and assign the most important ones first.) You will find that the more questions asked, the higher the quality of the answers. This is very important because the answers become action items for the next step in the process.

Step 4. Taking Action and Documenting Results

Taking action means simply taking the answers to the questions generated in the brainstorming process and turning them into action steps, such as determining timelines, allocating responsibilities, and following up. During this process, your team members will put their innovation training skills to the test. They will need to meet with those departments or individuals that will be affected by the proposed change, listen to their concerns, and give them an opportunity to participate in the innovation process. They will also need to document the results carefully. These activities are discussed in detail in Chapter 7, and sample documentation forms are included in the appendix.

Step 5. Reviewing and Following-Up

As emphasized throughout this book, the PBP approach must be a constant and continuous process. The final step, which is the subject of Chapter 8, recharges the dynamics of the process and triggers the next cycle, as the team reviews and follows up on the action plans. This process forces the team to discuss plan completion, results, contingencies, and corrective steps. The team must reapply the Questions Brainstorming and the Review and Follow-up steps to reach resolutions and initiate the next round of the process.

■ Summary

The Profit Building Process (PBP) is a five-step process for improving profitability and reducing costs. It offers innovative alternatives to workforce reduction and shows organizations how to give employees an opportunity to participate in a process that perpetuates cost reduction strategies and thereby sustains profit improvement.

The five steps of PBP are picking the team, preparing the team and the organization, brainstorming all the questions, taking action and documenting results, and reviewing and following up. Profit improvement can be learned, just like other management processes taught at any business school. Once managers are trained in identifying areas ripe for cost reduction, they will no longer need to fall back on layoffs. Instead, the company will be able to generate a long list of creative ways to continue to improve profits. The more people become involved in PBP, the greater and more diverse the ideas and solutions that emerge.

4 Choosing and Managing the Profit Building Team

> *What prodigious power a body of people can put forth when they all work at the same process, but the process differentiates and improves in their hands. Each gains skill and dexterity. They learn from each other, and the product is multiplied.*
> —WILLIAM GRAHAM SUMNER

Presently, the use of teams specifically to improve profit and loss is uncommon, despite management's widespread acquaintance with teams and what they can accomplish. The *Profit Building* approach shows managers how to select the right team members, organize meetings, and set concrete goals for optimal results in profit and loss management. When applied in proper sequence with the other steps to be discussed later in this book, the Profit Building Team (PBT) becomes the engine that drives profit building forward and perpetuates it.

When the right team is put into place, its creativity will impress you. The following is a small sample of some of the many creative questions generated by a team I worked with in 1994. A more inclusive list appears in Chapter 6.

Questions

- *Can a computerized labor management system schedule labor within 15-minute intervals?*

- *Can our part-time employees receive benefits through a professional employer organization (PEO)?*

- *Can we use incentives to encourage employees to decline insurance coverage if they are already carried on a spouse's plan?*

- *Do we have to agree to the standard 3% price increase passed on by most vendors every year?*

- *Can we pay trainees a lower rate?*

- *How are 401(k) administrative costs determined?*

- *How competitive are the 401(k) administrative fees?*

- *Can we negotiate the fees charged by fund managers who manage the mutual funds included in our portfolio?*

- *Does direct deposit of payroll save dollars?*

- *Can our company procure products and services at a lower cost by developing a purchasing co-op?*

- *Are there tax advantages in employing a targeted class of individuals?*

- *Are there tax credit programs that cover training costs?*

- *Are there any line items on the profit and loss statement that cannot be reduced?*

- *How can we control the purchase of premium gasoline for our entire fleet of 300 vehicles?*

- *How can we control maintenance costs for 300 vehicles?*

- *Is there anything we can do to control the cost of trash removal?*

- *How can technology help save us money?*

- *Can we negotiate bank charges?*

- *Instead of outsourcing, can we put some employees into business for themselves, with us as their first customer?*

- *Why do we carry excess property? What is the cost of carrying excess property?*

- *Are there less expensive ways to store our documents?*

- *Are there smarter ways to purchase office supplies? Can we consolidate all offices into one system and one vendor?*

- *If we show our vendors how to cut costs, will they pass on the savings to us?*

Our team went on to discover the answers to these questions, which then led to lucrative strategies for profit improvement and cost reduction. But it took the right mix of team members, training, and leadership to get these results. Following the guidelines below will help ensure that your organization will also put together a successful team.

■ Picking Your Team

An ideal Profit Building Team (PBT) can be defined as follows:

The PBT is a team of people who constitute a cross section of disciplines and are prepared for innovation. They will generate an endless list of questions, and the answers will fuel the perpetual, cyclical motion of the profit improvement machine in their organization.

The PBT has the following characteristics:

- It is a group of *no fewer than five and no more than eight people* who have been selected because they have demonstrated their ability to think "out of the box." The *cross-discipline, complementary, cross-sectional skills* they offer must cover operations, marketing, finance, information technology, human resources, telecommunications, and administration.

- Team members are *committed to reducing costs* within each line of the profit and loss (P&L) statement.

- Team members *must set performance goals* that will be easy to track and measure directly from future P&L statements.

- Team members must *hold themselves accountable* for the reduction of cost and the profit improvement directly associated with the team action steps.

- Team members *must meet on a regular basis* on the same day of the week, at the same time of day, and in the same place.

Each of these elements is an integral part of the PBT. A closer look reveals why they are so important to the team's success.

No Fewer Than Five, No More Than Eight

The PBT works best when it adheres to the "no fewer than five, no more than eight" guideline, because the issues associated with cost reduction require a sense of urgency, consensus, and action steps. A team larger than eight people slows down this process. A team smaller than five takes a narrow view, and not all key departments may be represented. However, five to eight people can reasonably commit themselves to a regular meeting schedule, can quickly become familiar with each other's abilities, is less likely to get bogged down in "politics," and requires fewer operating procedures. Most important, a team of this size is resilient and has the flexibility to shift its focus and change an approach when appropriate.

Please do not miss the critical point here. Size is an important characteristic of the PBT team. My recommendation to have no more than eight people on the team is made mainly because the primary task of the PBT is tending to the details, and this requires unrelenting focus. The Profit Building Process evolves over time, and each line item on the P&L is made up of a combination of activities that generate expense. Team members must isolate each activity and then analyze it in order to obtain, and then maintain, a reduced level of spending. A small team is faster on its feet, adapts more readily, experiences less turnover, and spends less time educating replacement members.

Out-of-the-Box Thinkers

The PBT requires team members who are out-of-the-box thinkers—people who tend to generate innovative ideas that push or reshape the envelope. Typically, when out-of-the-box thinkers come up against traditional, more conservative views, their inspirations are subjected to close scrutiny. More often than not, inspection reveals that these new ideas are on the cutting edge where change prevails and that they are highly appropriate solutions. This discovery is fundamental to the Profit Building Process.

The out-of-the-box thinkers are valuable players on your team; their creativity is contagious. At first, their unusual ideas may startle traditionalists. (In many organizations, it is wise to keep the traditionalist's viewpoint in mind when deciding how best to introduce the new idea.) But pondering the out-of-the-box thinkers' insights will eventually open the eyes of more conservative thinkers and challenge them to come up with some creative answers of their own. Author and manager Roger von Oech makes this point well in his book *A Whack on the Side of the Head:*

> We all need an occasional whack on the side of the head to shake us out of routine patterns, to force us to re-think our problems, and to stimulate us to ask the questions that may lead to other right answers.[1]

Your out-of-the-box thinkers may provide the "whack" your team needs to stimulate creative thinking. When you first form your team, you may also want to try some creativity exercises and brainteasers to get the creative juices flowing. Some out-of-the-box thinkers may be used to having their ideas stifled or rejected as too outlandish, so they may at first hesitate to share their thoughts. By engaging them in creative problem-solving exercises, you are encouraging them to unleash their creativity and sending the message that their innovative ideas are welcome. You are also laying the foundation for future creative thinking and problem solving, thus preparing your team to attack the real issues.

The involvement of out-of-the-box thinkers is so critical to the process that a consultant should be used if you find that your organization does not include team members with this ability.

Cross-Discipline, Complementary, Cross-Sectional Skills

When it comes to reducing cost on each line of the P&L statement, a team always outperforms an individual. The PBT requires the right chemistry—the proper mix of all functions within an organization—because cost reduction requires multiple skills and experiences, and because functional experts have the depth of knowledge needed to dig beneath the surface and ferret out opportunities for cost reduction. Most organizations miss opportunities to reduce cost by not including team members from all disciplines within the organization or business.

I must emphasize the importance of this "cross-discipline" approach. Including representatives from as many departments as possible creates a wide knowledge base. Each representative brings his or her unique perspective to the table, along with specialized knowledge and talents. You are creating a team of experts with inside knowledge on how the company operates, immediate acquaintance with its past and present performance, and priceless instincts about what methods would work best.

Another plus: Rather than focusing in just one or two areas, you have a whole organization to draw on for profit improvement. Small cost reductions in one or two departments might have little effect, but small reductions in *every* department in the company would translate into substantial savings. Think about it for a moment. If the human resources department could find ways to provide better benefits packages at lower cost, if marketing could achieve its goals of reach and frequency for fewer advertising dollars, if purchasing discovered better values, and so on, the total amount of money saved would spell a significant reduction in the organization's overall costs.

There is a tendency among managers to "put the blinders on" as they go about their daily activities. Absorbed in their own world, they become oblivious to the activities of other departments that may affect their own productivity. Following their daily routine, they may also fail to consider changes within their departments that could increase efficiency or cut waste. Just as it is easier to recognize someone else's faults than to acknowledge one's own, a team member from a different department may be quick to notice when another team member has become blind to the problems that exist right under her or his nose. PBT members quickly become "blinder-spotting" experts. This, coupled with their complementary skills and out-of-the-box thinking, leads to a team that is innovative, is creative, and covers the possibilities for cost reduction in every major department. This sort of team interaction is fundamental to the success of the Profit Building Process.

Commitment to Reducing Cost

Much has been written about the power of the commitment that evolves within successful teams. We know that nothing builds commitment more successfully than the people responsible for implementing the process being the ones that created it. People *want* to be successful. They *want* to see their ideas and action plans work. They *want* to reach their goals and enjoy the satisfaction of achievement. Recall the example of the Charmin paper plant. The team was fully committed to their goal of cutting costs without layoffs, and that commitment led to a number of innovative solutions. The answers are there, if only the team is dedicated to finding them.

The Profit Building Team must be committed to reducing costs and improving profits. This sole purpose must become the passion of the team. Commitment is a critical aspect of the PBT. Do not downplay it. In fact, my recommendation is to overplay this aspect because its power is real.

Stress this point by creating incentive programs for the Profit Building Team. Here are some examples:

- Create an incentive pool, using a percentage of the money saved by the PBT.

- Set a target amount to be saved. Dollars saved in excess of the target amount are split between the organization and the PBT members (for example, 20% of every dollar over the target might go to the team).

- Award extra vacation days to the PBT members upon their achievement of targets and goals.

- Recognize the team's achievements via publications, newsletters, or memoranda from senior management.

It is important to note that incentives do not need to be limited to financial rewards. Cruises, gift certificates, computers, and other items make good incentives. Also, you may want to reward on the basis of ideas generated, as well as money saved.

Performance Goals

What makes PBT so effective is that the process of setting performance goals is inherent in the concept. Because the goal of the team is to reduce costs from each line of the profit and loss statement, success can easily be measured by examining the next P&L. Once team members identify the line item dollars marked for reduction and put their plan in action, they can use each P&L statement as a monthly report card for tracking their progress.

Using the P&L as a report card for the team has several advantages:

1. P&L reports are produced on a regular basis.

2. The P&L is a familiar tool for reviewing results.

3. Using the P&L saves time because it eliminates the need to create a new tracking and measurement tool.

4. The P&L has broad readership at all levels of the organization. Therefore, the PBT members enjoy recognition and feedback from the rest of the organization.

5. P&L statements document the history of the company as well as the team's progress.

6. The P&L statement is a natural tool for measuring the Profit Building Process, because the main approach of PBP is to read between the lines of the P&L statement and identify opportunities for cost reduction. What better assessment tool than the P&L itself?

PBT Members Hold Themselves Accountable

The PBT holds a monthly review, which should be timed to follow the distribution of the P&L statement. During this review, individuals responsible for particular line items report on the action steps, the results, and any need for corrective action steps or new strategies. Each team member must report on his or her results. Then all team members are encouraged to express their views or offer suggestions. Team consulting is a good approach for generating new ideas or helping a team member who is falling behind on stated goals.

Emphasize this process by having each team member make a formal presentation about her or his individual performance. There is no better feeling than accomplishing what you say you are going to accomplish and reporting your own success! Conversely, for an individual whose results have fallen short of the goal or are not proceeding in the correct direction, making a presentation to the team is an opportunity to learn. The individual may be uncomfortable but can receive valuable feedback, suggestions, and ideas from the other members of the team. Working together, they will discover ways to remove the obstacles to the individual's success. Of course, most managers prefer the comfortable scenario and therefore will strive to achieve their stated goals. Individuals want to be seen as successful, and most will do whatever it takes to achieve success.

After each presentation, have all team members give feedback to the presenter in terms of how rapidly or slowly results are being obtained. It is my experience that teams who work together will, over a period of time, become more comfortable with feedback. Open and honest feedback brings the team together. Once the team is familiar with this process, the feedback becomes more useful. Giving peers a chance to offer suggestions or comments is powerful team building and will help raise team performance and cohesion to a new level.

PBT Members Must Meet on a Regular Basis

I recommend that the PBT meet every Friday at 2:00 P.M. Friday is a day when most managers are not traveling and are less likely to have conflicts with other obligations. Work schedules tend to become less rigid at this time in the afternoon. When the team is meeting each week, suggested action plans that require follow-up can be executed during the next week.

Regardless of what day or time you choose, be sure to make it consistent. Once team members get used to these scheduled meetings, their regular attendance will serve as a subtle confirmation of the continuity of the process.

■ PBT in Action

During 1985, while I was a regional vice president of Pizza Hut, a division of PepsiCo, I put together a team that consisted of representatives from all departments. Our goal was reducing costs. We were motivated by the fact that our financial plans had to demonstrate an improvement over our previous year's results. In this case, coming up with cost saving and/or profit improvement was particularly challenging, because our previous results had been very good. Furthermore, we had relied on new products to help increase revenues in previous years, and there were no new products on the drawing board. We had to be creative.

Complicating this situation was the fact that our team was new. Several promotions and transfers in key positions had left me with a team of people who had never worked together. There was an eclectic mix of personalities and working styles. Brion, from operations, was detail-oriented. Sharon, from marketing, was reticent because she had to take the heat when promotions were not effective. Lionel was very creative and understood various functions better than most finance people. And Laura, our human resources manager, had good people skills and an "in your face" attitude. Terry was our "out-of-the-box" thinker from franchise relations, whereas Bill, from restaurant development, was usually very quiet.

We had two problems: We had to find two million dollars, and our team was new. Before we could be creative and develop a plan, we had to overcome the fact that we were not used to working together.

At first we got nowhere. No two members could agree on an approach. Everyone was protective of his or her department, and we seemed to be at a stalemate. Then Laura from human resources came up with the idea of trying a unique team-building exercise. Every team member role-played the person to her or his right, making suggestions from that person's point of view.

It worked! We came up with a promotion that was almost too simple, though no one had proposed it before. We had all been wearing blinders, seeing only the needs of our own departments.

The promotion was called "just say cheese please." All employees were trained to encourage customers to order extra cheese on all pizzas sold. Successful execution of this tactic added incremental revenue dollars but was not perceived by customers as a price increase. It improved our food costs, leveraged our existing labor costs, and was seen by our customers as adding value.

Implementation of this idea was very successful. Not only did we achieve our financial goals but the team-building process that led to the generation of the idea also helped our team develop a stronger foundation. After that, our relationships grew and we continued to produce creative ideas and effective solutions. There was no question that our team's success was many times greater because we worked together.

■ Tips for Choosing and Managing Your Team

The most vital role of the team manager is exhibiting commitment to the goal and inspiring such commitment in others. The team manager must strongly believe in the importance of cost reduction and profit improvement, which, after all, should be a main focus of business. As team manager, you may want to share with your teammates the following words of Peter Drucker:

> The first performance requirement in a business is economic performance. Indeed, the first social responsibility for a business is to produce a profit adequate to cover the costs of capital and with them the minimum costs of staying in business. Adequate profitability alone can provide for the risks, growth needs, and jobs of tomorrow.[2]

All team members must be committed to profit improvement. As they complete daily tasks, manage their departments, and meet with co-workers, vendors, and customers, they should be continually on the lookout for opportunities to reduce costs and for obstructions to profitability. The team members' enthusiasm helps spread PBP throughout their respective departments and, eventually, throughout the organization. However, it all begins with the team manager's clear support of PBP.

When choosing your team members, you should not only look for out-of-the-box thinkers but also try to include as many *different* personality types as possible.

This may sound contrary to what many managers believe—if people share similar personalities, it is assumed that they are more likely to get along and thus facilitate a smooth-running team. However, it is for this very reason that the team may stagnate: A team of seven people who think alike will come up with only a limited number of discouragingly similar ideas, whereas a team of seven with different working and thinking styles is likely to generate a more diverse and innovative list. Paul Hersey and Kenneth Blanchard illustrate this point in *Management of Organizational Behavior:*

One of the reasons that hiring "likes" became popular is that it led to a more harmonious organization . . . .There will probably not be much conflict or confrontation. On the surface, this kind of screening appears to be very positive. Yet we have found that this approach can lead to organizational or management inbreeding, which tends to stifle creativity and innovation. To be effective in the long run, we feel that organizations need an open dialogue in which there is a certain amount of conflict, confrontation, and differing points of view to encourage new ideas and patterns of behavior so that the organization will not lose its ability to adjust to external competition.[3]

The manager's role is to bring people with diverse backgrounds and abilities together into a unified whole. The more diversity you have, the greater your chances of coming up with creative strategies for cost reduction. There may be some conflict within the team, but if managed effectively, the conflict should lead to a higher level of awareness among team members and to more out-of-the-box solutions. Focusing on the common goal of cost reduction should help to break down any barriers, and implementing the training program outlined in Chapter 5 will prepare your team for innovative thinking while helping to solidify relationships among them.

However, if you find your team is locked in a stalemate and can't seem to find an agreeable solution, try implementing a simple team-building exercise. Having team members role-play other team members during brainstorming has been very successful for me. You can also try humor, solving a riddle, or taking a short break. Anything that interrupts the current negative pattern, even momentarily, will usually get the team "over the hump" and on to more productive thinking.

■ Summary

PBT is a team of five to eight people who represent a cross section of departments and skills and who have the ability to think "out of the box." If you are a small business owner or department head, simply use a cross section of your existing group of employees.

After choosing the team, the team manager must make sure that each team member understands and is committed to the purpose of the team: reducing costs and improving profits in the organization. It is also the team manager's responsibility to set performance goals by line item on the profit and loss statement and to organize the regular weekly meetings.

Remember that the Profit Building Process is a team process. Its success depends on the team members' ability to work together. Communication, creative thinking, enlisting a cross section of departments and skills, and maintaining an unwavering focus on profit improvement are the basic elements, but a truly successful team will have the special synergy that sparks new thinking and innovative solutions. They will enjoy working together, form strong bonds, and feel pride in their achievements. Time will help cement the team and strengthen relationships, but the right training is also essential to getting the team off to the right start. The next chapter will describe team-building exercises and training and will explain how to prepare the team for the important task of managing change in the organization.

5 | Preparing Your Team and the Organization

Make thy Model before thou buildest; and go not too far
in it without due preparation.
—THOMAS FULLER

In 1987, I accepted a position with Imperial Savings, a
100-branch savings and loan organization. My title was senior vice
president, branch banking. I was responsible for making this 100-
branch network more profitable.

Before I accepted this position, I had been with Pizza Hut, Inc.,
where I was responsible for more than 1000 company-owned and
franchise-operated restaurants. Taking on Imperial's 100 bank
branches should have been a piece of cake. After all, these branches
were large facilities, made of marble, glass, and brass and fully
staffed by tellers who spent a third of their time serving customers.
But instead of my new job being easy, I found I had many obstacles
to overcome.

The branches were managed by vice presidents who had years of experience and tenure in the industry. I quickly learned that years of
experience and tenure do not necessarily translate into ease of transition or ready adoption of new ideas.

After firing off a slew of profit improvement ideas, my quiver was
empty of arrows to shoot at the inflated costs and inefficient procedures that plagued the organization—targets where I had always hit

bull's-eyes in the past. The words "profit improvement" did not have much meaning to upper management. It was as though the vice presidents didn't hear a word I was saying.

I decided to put together a cross-sectional team made up of branch vice presidents from across the state (California). I told the VPs to bring a list of ideas that, if implemented, would make them more successful in the organization. In doing so, I learned a valuable lesson. I already knew that individuals were difficult to change. Now I was to discover that without team preparation, a group of individuals is impossible to change.

The vice presidents' lists were all similar. They wanted control of their branches: marketing, human resources, training, and operational execution within their trade areas. To win their support, I showed them how they could get the control they wanted. Once I got on their "page" (not them on mine), their eyes and ears were opened. By working together, we generated the following ideas:

1. We developed a "franchise concept" for branch banking. In other words, we created procedures and processes that conceptually gave the vice presidents ownership of their branches (as though they were operating a franchise). They could keep a percentage of the "profits" generated from their individually planned and executed action steps.

2. We created a line of products—certificate of deposit, residential loan, credit cards, and fee income—and established revenue streams based on the financial impact these items would have on the organization. The result was that this revenue would be accounted as the top line of the individual branch that generated the product sale.

3. We created for each branch a P&L statement that included the fee income from the items mentioned in Step 2 as revenue and all specific branch expense items (fixed and variable).

4. We developed sales positions for selling various products at the branches.

5. We hired marketing personnel to design marketing plans.

6. *We developed a labor management system based on customer traffic within the individual branches.*

7. *We offered employee incentives for all employees in the branches. These incentives were based on performance measures that were easy to track and measure.*

8. *We designed employee recognition programs and rewarded outstanding employees in quarterly meetings.*

As this example shows, you may have the best ideas, changes, and innovations available, but your organization will not hear a word you say until the people are *prepared* to hear you. Your team must be prepared.

Most organizations are comfortable with picking and organizing the profit building team (PBT), because the activities are basic and straightforward. However, few organizations take the time to develop and train the team for the task, goals, or objectives they must accomplish. The following process, called PBP Innovation, is a tool that helps managers take this important step. It is designed to prepare the team for the process of managing unprecedented changes or innovation in the organization.

Think about your organization for a moment. How are routine situations handled? In most organizations, they are handled by applying pre-established procedures or processes. But a situation that is not so routine requires special handling. Typically, a non-routine situation or change is difficult to integrate because it requires time to develop the new procedures and processes necessary for its success. Also, non-routine change is more likely to encounter resistance from employees, who tend to be more comfortable following the current set of procedures and distrustful of the new ones. The longer a group works together with the same standard procedures, the more set in their ways they become. After all, team members and management constantly give and receive positive reinforcement for applying these standard procedures, so it is understandable that they might feel some confusion over suddenly being told to do things differently.

In *Management of Organizational Behavior,* authors Hersey and Blanchard make this point well:

While individual behavior is difficult enough to change, it becomes even more complicated when you try to implement change within groups or organizations. The leadership styles of one or two managers might be effectively altered, but drastically changing the level of follower participation throughout an entire organization might be a very time-consuming process. At this level you are trying to alter customs, mores, and traditions that have developed over many years.[1]

Such resistance makes it difficult to introduce new procedures, thus building "logjams" into the process of managing change or innovation within the organization.

In order to manage change or innovation throughout a business or organization, you must first prepare the organization for the change or innovation. This point is so critical that I have made organization and team preparation a key part of the Profit Building Process. Before discovering the necessity of this step, I spent many hours wondering why results were not on target for what I believed to be realistic timelines. The ideas were good, but good ideas were not enough; the organization was not prepared for change.

■ The Organizational Complexity Predictor

After much trial and error, I developed the Organizational Complexity Predictor (OCP). A copy of the OCP is included in the appendix. This tool can be used to measure the level of resistance to change that is currently present in your organization. The predictor is a simple questionnaire that rates various characteristics of the organization that can hinder change or innovation. A representative sample of employees need only take a few minutes to complete this questionnaire. Their combined answers are then used to identify areas for concern.

Because of the importance of assessing the complexity of the organization, I stress the need to use senior management to run interference during this step in the process. The following steps should be taken:

A. Meet with the senior executive and discuss the Profit Building Process. Explain why you need his or her support.

B. Discuss the importance of using the Organizational Complexity Predictor to assess how difficult or easy it will be to manage change in the organization.

C. Seek a memorandum signed by the senior executive asking every employee to complete the questionnaire.

D. Distribute the questionnaire and memorandum, including a specific date when the questionnaire must be returned.

E. Analyze the data. Ideally, you would want everyone in the organization to complete the questionnaire. However, 50 percent of a team, department or company is adequate representation.

F. Identify items that are a cause for concern. Any item with a rating of Low to Average, or 4 and below, signals a problem area.

G. Once the Low to Average items are identified, I recommend immediately developing action steps to address these areas. Managers should openly communicate the results and commit themselves to addressing these issues.

Complexity Survey Summary

The following are actual results of using the Organizational Complexity Predictor in an organization. Please note that this summary of the survey is a basic action plan for addressing areas of concern.

1. *In the organization, is there a continuous need for various departments to work together in order for a product or service to be delivered?*

   The need for departments to work together was rated High by the organization.

2. *Is the organization strategic in its action(s)?*

   The organization received an Average rating on whether it is strategic in its actions.

3. *Is there frequent turnover in middle and upper management?*

    The organization received a Low rating on whether there is frequent turnover in middle and upper management. This is an area to discuss.

4. *Is there frequent turnover in the lower levels of the organization?*

    The organization received an overall rating of Low to Average on turnover at lower levels. This is an area to discuss.

5. *Are new ideas quickly adopted and diffused throughout the organization?*

    The organization received an overall rating of Low to Average on speed of adoption of new ideas. This looks like an area for concern.

6. *Is the generation of new ideas encouraged in the organization?*

    The organization received an overall rating of Average to High on whether generation of new ideas is encouraged.

7. *Does the organization have resources set aside to reward the generation of new ideas?*

    The organization received an overall rating of Low to Average on resources to reward new ideas. Combined with the outcome for Question 6, these results suggest that new ideas are encouraged in intangible ways but not in tangible ways. This looks like an area for concern.

8. *Does the organization communicate a wish to generate new ideas from its employees?*

    The organization received an overall rating of Average on communication of a wish to generate new ideas.

9. *Are new procedures easily rolled out and implemented in the organization?*

    The organization received an overall rating of Low on rolling out new procedures easily. This looks like the number 1 area for concern.

10. *Does the organization use project planning when it undertakes a major project?*

    The organization received an overall rating of Average to High on use of project planning. This looks like good news.

11. *Are "end users" of new procedures given the opportunity to provide input before the development of these new procedures?*

    The organization received an overall rating of Low to Average on giving end users an opportunity to provide input into the development of new procedures. This looks like an area for concern.

12. *Are "end users" given the opportunity to modify or reinvent existing procedures?*

    The organization received an overall rating of Low to Average on giving end users an opportunity to modify or reinvent existing procedures. Combined with the outcome for Question 11, these results suggest that people see more opportunity to fix new procedures in practice than to get them right to start with.

13. *Is top management committed to change and innovation?*

    The organization received an overall rating of Average, but with a large symmetric range of opinion (lack of consensus) about whether top management is committed to change and innovation. The lack of a common perception (or experience) looks like an area for concern, even though the overall rating is Average.

14. *Does the organization learn from its mistakes?*

    The organization received an overall rating of Average on whether it learns from its mistakes.

15. *Is senior management hired from within the organization?*

    The organization received an overall rating of Average on whether senior management is hired from within the organization.

16. *Does senior management solicit new ideas from within the organization?*

The organization received an overall rating of Low to Average on whether senior management solicits new ideas from within the organization. This is an area for concern.

17. *Are there innovation champions within the ranks of senior management?*

The organization received an overall rating of Average to Low, but the high rate of no response may be de facto testimony of many others who do not know any champions but do not want to deny that there are some unknown to them. This should be considered an area for concern.

18. *Does the organization have an aggressive e-strategy for planning e-commerce and e-tactics?*

The organization received an overall rating of Average in this area.

19. *Does the organization give cash incentives for generation of new ideas?*

The organization received an overall rating of Average cash incentives.

20. *Does the organization have an aggressive program for attracting female and minority employees and vendors?*

The organization received an overall rating of Average on diversity.

Questionnaire Summary

The perceived areas of concern are

- Ease of rolling out new ideas (worst median rating and number 1 area for concern).
- Speed of adoption of new ideas and availability of resources to reward those who generate them.
- Whether end users are given the opportunity to offer input on new procedures before they are adopted.

Less clear-cut but possible areas of concern are

- Whether top management is committed to change.
- Whether innovation champions exist within senior management.

Action Steps

✔ Develop a procedure for changing the way new ideas are rolled out and implemented in the organization. (Q9)

✔ Develop a procedure for finding a more effective way for the organization to adopt and diffuse new ideas. (Q5)

✔ Develop a procedure for giving end users the opportunity to provide input on new procedures before their adoption. (Q11)

✔ Discuss how top management can better communicate commitment to change and innovation. (Q13)

✔ Review the low results on management and employee turnover. Determine whether these results are creating an organization that is difficult to change. (Q3, Q4)

■ PBT Preparation

The first task of the newly formed PBT is to review the results of the OCP, an assessment of the organization's ability to handle change. This "snapshot" will indicate how easy or difficult the process of managing change, innovation, new ideas or procedures will be. The more complex the task of managing change, the more preparation the team needs.

Assessing the team and the organization's ability to change is the easy part. The challenge is setting the stage for change to take place. Because change is often seen as threatening, people naturally try to avoid the process by putting on blinders. This and other defense mechanisms make change almost impossible to manage in an organization that is unprepared for it. The paragraphs that follow describe several ways to prepare your organization for change or for adopting innovations. (In a large organization, managers and department heads implement these methods. In smaller companies, the CEO, vice president, or business owner may be involved. Adjust the process to suit your company's needs.)

A. Direct Confrontation

B. Audit the Entire Process

C. Regular Surveys

D. Customer Meetings

E. Vendor Discussions

F. Outside Hires

G. Board Member Exposure

H. Special Communication Improvements

I. Training

J. Process Review

K. Incentives and Contests

Direct Confrontation

Confront the entire organization and discuss how the employees' resistance is making the introduction of innovation and/or change very difficult. It is appropriate to discuss the ramifications of what would happen if the planned innovation did not take place. What would be the shortcomings of the organization? What steps will need to be taken if those planned innovations do not occur?

Think about your existing organization. What type of impact would a meeting with senior management have where the subject was a report card on how the company managed change? If your CEO, business owner, or department head called the employees together to communicate the need for everyone to become more open to change, innovations, and new ideas, would the feedback be positive? I believe that this type of communication *would* be positive and would start to move the organization toward being more innovative and creative.

Have key members of the organization complete the Organizational Complexity Predictor and discuss the average score. (The predictor is helpful because it gives you some solid information to work with—the numbers don't lie.) In a large organization, I recommend including the senior management, all department heads, and a cross section of the workforce. In a smaller company, all employees might participate. At various meetings, directly confront the entire organization with the results, from top executives down to the workforce. Discuss examples of past attempts to implement innovations or changes. Solicit feedback from these groups about what went right and what did not. It has been my experience that direct confrontation results in a higher level of awareness about the personality of the organization and the factors that might be impeding change. Direct confrontation forces individuals or groups to realize that something they are doing is preventing change from taking place.

Audit the Entire Process

It is always appropriate for management to audit various procedures within the organization. During this process, discuss any possible changes in procedures with the people who will be affected. Get them involved in the process, soliciting their ideas and input. This is also a good time to focus on and address any resistance to change that may be lurking within the group. Bring these feelings out in the open for discussion and clarification, and explore possible action steps for minimizing resistance.

At this meeting you may also discuss proposed innovations and the best ways to adopt them. The timing is good because people are open to accepting innovations or improved processes in this environment.

Regular Surveys

Organizations should develop various surveys for continually checking on the level of satisfaction or dissatisfaction of their employees. Once the survey is complete, score the results and discuss them with a cross section of the employees who took the survey. The results of the discussions should be documented, along with appropriate action steps that will be taken, and this information should be sent to the entire organization.

When surveys are administered regularly, employees become more comfortable with participating in them. As the percentage of employees taking surveys grows, the feedback provided to management becomes more accurate, because people feel that they can communicate via the process and that their communications are heard.

Customer Meetings

Listen to your customers. Listening to customers will reveal a deeper understanding of the characteristics of the organization and how it has become resistant to change and innovation.

The need to listen has been brought up in many management books on the market today. In *The Service Edge*, Ron Zemke writes,

> The priority today is to continuously and carefully listen to customers, understand what they're saying as it applies to the business of serving them, and respond creatively to what they tell you. [2]

Create a forum where several key customers can participate and provide feedback about the organization's products and/or services. Such meetings yield excellent feedback about the logjams of resistance that prevent smooth transactions from taking place. Developing an ear for these types of logjams can help managers understand the personality of their own organization.

Vendor Discussions

Hold regularly scheduled meetings with vendors. This may be done by the sales staff, by managers, or by the CEO, depending on the size of the company. Like the customer forums, these discussions should explore possible logjams that might be preventing business transactions from taking place. There is a tendency in some organizations to treat vendors a bit differently from customers, but I believe that for this purpose they should be approached similarly. Vendors can make suggestions on how the organization can improve or innovate. There may be new strategic alliances that would benefit the organization if it were open to change. Keep in mind that your vendors are also vendors to other companies—possibly your competitors—and that they themselves are looking to change, innovate, and improve profitability. Regular meetings with vendors provide another avenue for exploring the personality of the organization. Once regular meetings are established, the organization will get a feel for how it will manage change internally.

Outside Hires

Establish hiring ratios that emphasize both internal promotions and external hires. Organizations should determine what percentage of the workforce is to be hired from the outside. As an example, let's say that 40 percent of job openings should be filled by new hires and 60 percent should be filled via promotion from within. A percentage at this level permits an influx of new ideas from the outside, while allowing the organization to keep what has made it strong: its history, experience, background, business knowledge, customer knowledge, product knowledge, approaches to profit improvement, and approaches to customer satisfaction—all of the important aspects of the business that have developed into core competencies. It is important to balance internal and external personnel. When an organization promotes only from within, the atmosphere grows stagnant. Consequently, it is less likely to be open to new ideas or change.

Board Member Exposure

Generally speaking, organizations do not utilize board members as well as they should. In many organizations, the board of directors could be more visible. Most board members have experience in many different organizations—the combined backgrounds of 5 to 8 board members should include 40 or 50 different companies—and possess skills that are important to the organization. While I was president of U.S. Autoglas, our board was made up of many talented individuals. Their backgrounds included manufacturing, food service, retail, big-six accounting, consulting, and law, to name a few. Their vast experience made them a good sounding board for exploring new ideas. We kept them involved in the company on a regular basis. Consequently, they were more aware of all aspects of the organization and were able to help us innovate at critical times.

Of course, the size of the board and their involvement will vary with the organization. The managers of a smaller company can benefit from inviting their board to join them at regular staff meetings. A large corporation with numerous board members may need to hold special meetings to keep the board involved and up-to-date.

With so much valuable experience behind them, board members should not be ignored. They bring a fresh set of eyes and a wealth of knowledge to the strategic aspects of the business.

With additional exposure, board members can assist the senior management and give more appropriate feedback on the internal workings of the organization, especially in terms of managing change. Have board members meet with as many employees as possible. Once they understand the issues in more detail, get them involved in strategic discussions with senior management on managing change and innovation. Let them explore the issues that may arise as the changes are implemented throughout the organization. Take advantage of your board members' knowledge and experience; they have probably faced similar issues and may suggest some valuable solutions.

Special Communication Improvements

Roll out a complete internal Public Relations campaign. The campaign's objective is to discuss change and innovation, explain why it is important, and explore how everyone can help make change and innovation take place. Company newsletters should emphasize innovation, and several memos on change should go out on a weekly basis. Focus on the complexity of managing change. Build regularly scheduled meetings into the communication process so that senior management can discuss change and innovation with employees and solicit their feedback.

Training

Challenge the training department to come up with various training programs that address innovation management. These programs should be organized, tracked, and monitored, and they should be beneficial to every employee in the organization. Create a company-wide "people development process" that stresses how each individual plays an important role in making innovation successful. Encourage employees to come up with changes and innovations of their own and to join others in making innovation a reality.

Employees are more enthusiastic about change and innovation when they have made a contribution to the process. In *Your Signature Path*, Geoffrey Bellman writes,

> Contribution is one of the great human reasons for work. In volunteer organizations, in the social services, and in politics, the opportunity to contribute to the larger community draws volunteers . . . . People making money through their work are not precluded from this satisfaction.[3]

This type of continual training and development will make each future change easier to implement in the organization.

Process Review

The organization should continue to look at all processes and procedures. All managers should have the task of reviewing procedures and processes in the organization on a regular basis, checking for logjams that might be preventing change or innovation from taking place. Managers should also include all levels of employees in this process of review. These individuals have been working with the procedures and can provide feedback on how to improve them. Regular process review makes the innovation or change process easier to execute.

Incentives and Contests

Use incentives and contests to keep the focus on change and innovation. Look for opportunities to set goals that are related to change and innovation management. For example, reward the first department to implement the new process successfully, or give incentives to employees for adopting the changes you outline for them. Be sure to include employees at all levels of the organization, making innovation a company-wide goal.

As you can see by now, preparing the organization for change is no easy task. Its complexity is probably the reason why this important step is often overlooked. But it is vital to the success of PBP, and if you follow the approach just described, you will have a much easier time of making innovation take hold within the organization.

■ Managing Change

You have used the Organization Complexity Predictor to assess the organization's resistance to change. You have become acquainted with some tools that will help you prepare management and the workforce to embrace (or at least accept) changes. Through training and internal PR programs, you have started to create a more open-minded and creative environment ready to implement your innovations. Now what?

To smoothly manage the changes to come, the PBT needs training in innovation management. Organizational scientists have developed several theories and empirical observations about the topic of managing change and innovation throughout organizations. Here you will find some practical suggestions on how to use this information in managing the process of innovation. Before members of the team can begin to understand how to manage change or innovation, they must first learn some basic information about the development of innovation and about its adoption by individuals.

If you have ever studied the excellent work of some organizational scientists, you may agree that their insight into the complicated "under-current" that drives the dynamics of teams has much merit. My management experience validates these scientists' findings and I have attempted to digest their theories into a step-by-step process, making them "live" and useful in the organization. Step 2 of PBP is built on their theories.

■ Basic Innovation and Adoption

I have learned that there are three steps to the innovation process as originated by Everett Rogers: idea invention, idea development, and idea adoption/diffusion. *Idea invention* consists of recognizing the need for change and researching these needs for clearer understanding. *Idea development* includes design and commercializing, and *adoption/diffusion* means adopting the innovation and then marketing it, distributing it, and promoting it. Because most businesses are always faced with the need to reduce costs and improve profits, the idea invention stage is pre-established.

Training is a critical step in the innovation and adoption process, and essential for your profit building team. Too often we carefully choose a team for a specific purpose, only to start them off on the wrong foot by leaving them unprepared for meeting the challenges that lay ahead. After investing much time and thought in selecting the right team members, ensure their success by equipping them with the tools and strategies they need to succeed. Without training, team members may fail to understand their purpose, become frustrated with the process and eventually give up on profit building altogether. Appropriate training is a small investment that will build relationships, sharpen skills, and clarify the team's purpose. Consequently, your organization will see the benefit of larger returns.

The PBP training program has several important objectives, including:

- Introducing some of the key aspects of innovation management.

- Providing awareness of the need for change (in this case, the need for cost reduction and profit improvement).

- Teaching PBT members how to persuade the rest of the organization of the need for change.

- Showing team members how to evaluate the best methods for introducing change.

- Enabling team members to implement the change throughout the organization.

- Helping team members recognize current problems in the P&L statement.

- Demonstrating why the PBT will be successful.

- Training team members to develop specific plans for greater success.

The following program contains outcomes, objectives, agendas, activities, assignments, timelines, discussions, and summaries. You do not need to be an experienced trainer to conduct this program—I have seen all levels of management execute it successfully.

The program is designed into three sessions, to be held on three separate days. I recommend holding the sessions on three Fridays in a row. This way, assignments can be completed between sessions.

This training program will give the team leader and team members the confidence to start what will be a new process in most organizations. The PBT will also obtain what most teams miss—the ability to successfully implement a new idea within an organization. Remember that the effectiveness of your training program has a direct impact on the kinds of results your organization can expect to achieve. Take your time with training. It is not about speed. It is not about quickly completing the steps. In real estate, we often hear the phrase, "location, location, location." In PBP, I want you to think "training, training, training."

PBT Innovation Management Training Program

Instructor: Team Leader
Participants: PBT Members

Outcomes: By the end of the training session, the participants will be able to:

- Describe the steps of the innovation process.
- Explain why the organization has a need to focus on cost reduction and profit improvement.
- Persuade the rest of the organization of the need for change.
- Evaluate alternatives and determine the best method for introducing the change.
- Implement the change throughout the organization.
- Recognize the current problems in the P&L statement.

Agenda: Session 1

Time Frame	Description of Activities
15 minutes	Make any necessary introductions. Review the agenda. Review the objectives.
35 minutes	Large-Group Discussion: PBT…discuss the purpose of the team, the outcomes, and the reasons why each person wants to be on the team. (Assigning members to read Chapters 1–4 of *Profit Building* could help here.) *Expectation Exchange:* On a flip chart, list the things the team leader hopes to accomplish via this training session. Then list the PBT members' expectations. Discuss the similarities and differences. Agree on the expectations.

Make sure each team member participates. This will help introduce the open communication process so vital to PBP.
Note: This discussion connects the team's purpose to larger organizational goals and innovation activities.

40 minutes   Small-Group Discussion:
The basic innovation process.

Break the team into three small groups. Each group is responsible for developing an example of one of the steps of the innovation process.

Group 1: Idea invention (Step 1)
Group 2: Idea development (Step 2)
Group 3: Idea adoption/diffusion (Step 3)

Each group should read the paragraph on basic innovation and adoption in this chapter. Then have each group develop its own definition of its assigned step, using real examples from their own experience. Allow 15 minutes.

15 minutes   After the 15-minute period is up, ask the group to answer the following questions (these should be written on a flip chart).

- What is the purpose of your step in the process?
- What is the purpose of this phase of the process?
- How is this phase related to other steps in the process?
- What are the benefits to the organization?
- How can this team help the organization realize the benefits of understanding the steps of the innovation process?

15 minutes	Large-Group Discussion: The small groups present their answers to the team.
10 minutes	Large-Group Discussion: ■ What are the similarities among the three small-group discussions? ■ What are the unique elements of the presentations? ■ What are the clues that identify the steps of the model? Summarize the main points.
15 minutes	Individual Reflection…Case for Change: What are the reasons why the organization needs to focus on improving profits? Silently, participants identify the reasons for making the change effort in the organization at this time. Participants record their answers on adhesive-backed cards. Acknowledge the participants who have identified the most reasons, the most outrageous reasons, and the most compelling reasons. Post the reasons for change under two headings: ■ Most Outrageous Reasons for Change (Have a little fun here!) ■ Most Compelling Reasons for Change
15 minutes	Large-Group Discussion: Identify 3–5 reasons for the change effort that can be used to communicate the rationale for change to others in the organization.
20 minutes	Pair Discussion: Participants pair together to present their understanding of the discussion. Each participant makes a 2-minute presentation to his or her partner:

- What is the purpose of PBT?
- Why should the organization improve its profits?
- How will the PBT affect the organization's profitability and efforts at innovation?

Provide feedback to the partner:

- What was communicated well?
- What would make the presentation more effective?

15 minutes	The team leader should pull the group back together and make sure the purpose of the PBT is clear. The team leader should review Chapters 1–3 for ideas.

Session 1 Assignment:
Ask PBT members to set up meetings with members of their departments to discuss the purpose of the PBT.

Close the session.

Agenda: Session 2

Time Frame	*Description of Activities*
10 minutes	Review the outcomes of the training for the PBT members (listed on the first page of the training program).
	Discuss the last assignment. Ask, "How did your departments react when you told them about the PBT?"
	The team leader should watch for resistance, barriers, or other signs of opposition to the idea of profit building.
60 minutes	Large-Group Discussion: How can the PBT do each of the following?

- Become aware of the *need for change* (cost reduction and profit improvement)
- *Persuade* the rest of the organization
- *Evaluate* alternatives and determine the best method for introducing change
- *Implement* the change throughout the organization

The team leader should choose four individuals to lead the four segments of the discussion (need for change, persuade, evaluate, implement). Make sure everyone is actively participating.

30 minutes	Group Exercise: Divide the team into two groups. Ask each group to develop an action plan for implementing cost reduction and profit improvement throughout the organization. What steps would they take? Plan Review: Have each group present its plan.
10 minutes	Close the session.

Agenda: Session 3

Time Frame	*Description of Activities*
10 minutes	Review Session 2: Ask, "Why will the PBT be successful in implementing change?" Post answers for the group.
30 minutes	Pair Discussion: Identify the line items on the P&L statement that are of concern. Discuss with your partner the additional research required to understand each issue and steps to resolve it. (For this activity, the team leader must pass

out a recent copy of the P&L statement. It
may be necessary to review it in front of
the team.)

30 minutes   Large-Group Discussion:
Have each pair present to the group their
discussion of the issues that their examina-
tions of the P&L statement suggests. The
following items should be discussed:

- Issues that arise through examination of
  the P&L statement
- Additional research (tools and approaches)
- Steps required (to address issues)

Identify additional resources for people
with mutual issues with the P&L statement.

15 minutes   Double Reversal:
Have groups of four people brainstorm answers to the following question: "What do
we need to do to ensure that the PBT fails?"

After the group finishes brainstorming,
it should identify the factors that are
most likely to cause the team to fail.
Acknowledge the group with the most
responses.

15 minutes   Large-Group Discussion:
Engage in contingency planning. That is,
conduct a discussion on the reasons for failure that were identified by the group.

20 minutes   Small Groups:
Ask each group to develop plans to combat
the potential causes of failure that have
been identified. What needs to be done to
ensure that the team does not fail? Each
small group presents its ideas to the team.

30 minutes	Senior Executive Discussion: Invite a senior executive to the meeting room to listen to the plans the small groups have developed and learn how the group plans to address issues that arise through examination of the P&L statement.
	The group should discuss with the executive its concerns and any remaining issues.
10 minutes	Conclude the session by summarizing the main points and the importance of the PBT's work.

■ Summary

In order to manage change or innovation in the organization, you must first prepare the organization for change. This is one of the main points of the Profit Building Process. The Organizational Complexity Predictor is a valuable tool for measuring the level of resistance to change present within an organization. It identifies specific areas that will need to be addressed before change can be implemented effectively. A direct approach is often the best way to overcome resistance to change. Confront the organization head-on, discussing the problems that exist with the status quo and the ramifications if change does not take place.

During this process it is equally important to prepare the Profit Building Team; its members are the ones responsible for implementing change throughout the organization. The team must be made aware of the basic Innovation/Adoption/ Diffusion model, and they must be committed to the purpose of the team. They must become aware of the need for change (cost reduction and profit improvement), must be able to *persuade* the rest of the organization, must *evaluate* alternatives and determine the best methods, and must *implement* the change throughout the organization.

Preparing the team and the organization for accepting and implementing change is a lengthy process, but it is also a necessary one. Countless good ideas have failed simply because the organization was not prepared to accept them. If you follow the process described in this chapter, you will have laid the groundwork for making effective and meaningful change within the organization.

6 Generating Creative Solutions by Asking *All* the Questions

When we arrived at the question, the answer is already near.
—Ralph Waldo Emerson

In 1983 I became a vice president at Pizza Hut, Inc., a division of PepsiCo, Inc. This was an exciting and eventful achievement for me that included company stock, financial rewards, and recognition. One of the perks I received was an opportunity to go to the corporate office for a three-day management program the vice presidents referred to as "finishing school." Although I did not know it at the time, this experience was to make an impression on me that would help shape both my career and the thinking that came to underlie the Profit Building Process (PBP).

The highlight of this program was a high-powered meeting with the CEO and a few top members of his staff. In this meeting, vice presidents from various divisions across the country jockeyed for position, each hoping to make a positive impression on the CEO and his team. The format was a sort of oral exam; the CEO would ask a vice president a variety of questions, and one's answers could result in either personal glory or public humiliation. The atmosphere was tense, the competition so thick you could cut it with a jackhammer.

I was both excited and nervous about participating in this event. I had no idea what kind of questions might be asked. In preparing for this session, I decided to ask my own questions of as many of the more seasoned vice presidents as possible.

I pursued the others with my list of questions. What topics were usually discussed? What are the hot buttons? Are the questions financial or strategic? Will I be asked about marketing or operations? Then, on the basis of the answers I received, I did my homework.

My preparation paid off, and when my moment came, I was ready. During my "fifteen minutes of fame," I was able to dazzle the CEO with my knowledge of marketing, planning, and administration, and I even asked him several questions of my own. Although I was "the new guy," I quickly earned the respect of upper management. But more important, the information I had gleaned by asking questions pointed me in the right direction and helped prepare me to meet the challenges that lay ahead in my new position. I continue to use this process today and have made it Step 3 of the PBP.

My point here is not to brag about my achievements, but to underscore the power of asking questions. Prior to my investigations, I knew little about the topics I was about to be quizzed on by the CEO. However, by asking numerous questions and doing some research, I was able to come across as well informed.

But let's take the power of questions a step further. The CEO of this multi-billion-dollar corporation made this group of experienced, elite vice presidents sweat and squirm by simply asking questions.

This experience indelibly impressed upon my mind the power of asking questions, and this process has become a tool that I use repeatedly in business to glean the information I need to make sound decisions. In this chapter, I want to speak further about why I believe in the power of questions.

Think for a moment of the many times when you are asked questions in your life. Tests in grade school and college, SAT scores, CPA exams, interview questions—all determine whether you pass or fail. These questions are opportunities to display your knowledge. They are problems seeking answers. When I am solving a problem, each question I ask takes me one step closer to reaching a solution.

I have noticed that organizations and the management processes that drive them tend to shy away from questions. There seems to be an unspoken rule that too many questions are bad and that therefore, many questions get asked only in the final stages of a process. We have all been there: a training program, a seminar, a business meeting, or even an interview where at the end of the session we hear, "Are there any questions?" or "Let's hold questions until the end." There may be any number of reasons why this happens, but it nearly always serves to confine creative interaction and denies what could otherwise have been a rich exchange of ideas.

In business cultures, asking questions seems to have a negative connotation. Questions are perceived as antagonistic, confrontational challenges of authority. Organizations also seem to be more interested in gathering information, a process wherein results are predictable, than in encouraging new questions, because the answers require more time and energy to process.

Questions should be encouraged at all times and at all levels within the organization. The people who speak up and position themselves as the authority on a particular topic seem to get all the credit, attention, support, control, and key roles in the organization. But I believe that the quiet majority have more to bring to the problem-solving party than the few who have won us over by assuming the leadership role. We need the participation of everyone in the group to provide a broad range of ideas, potential solutions, and action steps to resolve the business problems of today.

Ironically, the people who could contribute the most to profitability improvement are often the first to receive the pink slip in the name of cost reduction. Faced with the need to reduce cost or improve profit, many managers turn to layoffs to meet their stated goals. Typically, those laid off are the same employees who for years produced the products, delivered the services, and satisfied the customers. They are the employees who not only know the answers to the cost reduction questions but also know how to improve the overall process necessary to achieve success for the organization. If management will provide an environment in which employees can question the entire process, and will ask them to develop the action steps necessary to deliver that 10 or 20 percent cost reduction, it will get results. The first step is to discuss the business situation with a group of employees so that everyone is clear on the objective. Then let those employees come up with possible solutions to generate improvements in profit without massive layoffs. This is what PBP is all about.

■ From Questions to More Questions . . . To Solutions

Questions Brainstorming is a new approach to brainstorming. Unlike the traditional management problem-solving approach, this process involves brainstorming the *questions*, rather than trying to come up with immediate answers and short-term solutions. I have found that the process of brainstorming questions produces an endless list of questions that, in turn, stimulates creativity and produces the fuel necessary to keep the process of continual improvement going. In PBP, the answers to these questions form the framework for constructing future action plans. The traditional practice of brainstorming for answers generates fewer ideas and (consequently) fewer solutions.

Example A—Traditional Method of Brainstorming

Call a group of employees together from various departments in your organization. Tell them that the goal is to come up with action steps to reduce costs or improve profits. Have the group start the brainstorming process by listing, on a flip chart, the action steps that could lead toward profitability improvement. Give the team a copy of the most recent profit and loss statement as a reference. Typically, a few employees will take the initiative to call out some possible solutions, and the flip chart starts to look like this:

1. Increase revenue.
2. Improve marketing.
3. Reduce labor costs.
4. Reduce benefits costs.
5. Cut travel and entertainment.
6. Eliminate unnecessary departments.
7. Improve productivity.
8. Reduce communication costs.
9. Reduce utility costs.

These items are then prioritized, and action steps put in place. A person is assigned responsibility for the various action steps, and corrective actions are taken.

Example B—Questions Brainstorming

Call a group of employees together from various departments in your organization. Tell them the goal is to come up with a list of questions whose answers will become action steps to reduce costs or improve profits. Have the employees start the process by listing on a flip chart only the questions—no potential answers or solutions. Give the team a copy of the most recent profit and loss statement as a reference. At this point, a different process begins to take shape. All employees are participating. Everyone is asking questions because they don't have to come up with the answers. The few people who took the initiative to start the process in Example A are now joined by most of the others, because this is a less stressful context for participation.

Think of the child who continues to ask her or his parents, "Why? Why? Why?" The parents eventually get frustrated, because the child is forcing them to become more creative with their answers. Even the most intelligent parents quickly reach their intellectual limit in a discussion with a small child. The process of questions brainstorming overcomes this drawback.

It demands no answers but generates an endless list of questions. The flip chart for Example B will look very different from the traditional list generated in Example A:

1. How is revenue generated?
2. What new revenue generation activities have been tried?
3. How many marketing dollars are spent each year? Why?
4. Why do we have this specific cost?
5. Do we need this cost?
6. What are some alternatives to what we have been doing?
7. Were we charged a proper amount for this service?
8. What is the price of this service? Why?
9. When was the last time this price was negotiated?
10. What do similar companies pay for this service?
11. Why are we paying more?
12. Can we buy this service or product from someone else?
13. Can we outsource this activity?
14. Can a consultant do these tasks?
15. How do we know that we are being charged the proper amount?
16. How do we know whether our price is competitive?
17. Do we take price increases every year? Why?
18. Etc., etc., etc.

You can see how the list could be endless. The questions are then prioritized, and each is assigned to an individual to seek answers. Once the answers are found, the action plans can be developed.

Managers will notice a significant change in the quality of team members' participation, and in the level of creativity in the questions, as the group generates the endless list of questions from which answers and solutions can be gleaned. The process of thinking about questions provides the framework for the answers, and these, in turn, help construct the action items for the cost reduction or profit improvement process.

■ Questions Brainstorming in Action

It is amazing how quickly asking questions can generate results. While senior vice president at Envirotest Systems, Inc., I introduced this process as a means of discovering solutions to the company's profitability woes. Envirotest was a $170-million provider of automotive vehicle emissions testing throughout the United States and Canada. At the time I took over the operation, the business was achieving a 26% EBITDA (earnings before interest, taxes, depreciation, and amortization). Its $44 million of cash flow was not enough to cover bank interest, depreciation, and corporate overhead. Although the managers who made up my newly formed team had never worked together before, during our first meeting they were able to generate a list of viable solutions just by asking questions. Together, we came up with the following list of questions regarding our cash flow problem:

- *Why doesn't the organization train its managers in financial management?*
- *Why does the corporate office run our programs? Why not give us complete responsibility?*
- *Can we develop a way for managers to track and control labor?*
- *Why do we have so many duplicate support positions across the country?*
- *Do we need safety training?*
- *Can we offer incentives to managers?*
- *Can each office become responsible for the lobbying interests in its states?*
- *Why are corporate consultants making changes to our programs?*
- *Can we develop ancillary products to grow revenue?*

- *Can we become responsible for managing our individual state partners?*
- *Etc., etc., etc.*

After we addressed these and other questions with the corporation, we developed the following partial list of action steps:

- *We assigned the training department the task of creating a two-course profit and loss training program (basic and advanced).*
- *We changed the program manager's title to general manager, to express the general managerial functions of the position, and included profitability improvement and ongoing accountability among his responsibilities.*
- *We assigned operations the task of creating a computerized labor management system to help more than 300 managers schedule their part-time labor force in 15-minute increments.*
- *We created regional marketing, finance, and human resources managers and upgraded these positions to attract stronger candidates.*
- *We put into place action plans for reducing accidents and consequently reduced worker's compensation costs.*
- *We developed cash reconciliation programs to save labor during shift changes and station-closing procedures.*
- *We created salary administration programs with "hire-in" rates, with adjustments based on tenure and completion of training.*

Additional action plans addressed revenue enhancement, utility usage, property tax reevaluation, and employee incentive programs for cost reduction. The net effect of these actions over a 3-year period generated an EBIDTA improvement of $44 million to an $88 million cash flow, or a 52% EBITDA.

As this example shows, brainstorming questions is essential to PBP. It provides an endless set of questions that fuels the continuous improvement process, and it should develop into a core competency within the organization. Note also that prior to this exercise, this team had not worked together specifically to improve profitability. Most of us were new in the organization and the industry. We asked questions whose answers became action steps and later cost reduction ideas.

■ Start Asking Questions

Once a team is trained in and familiar with the Questions Brainstorming approach, team members become very comfortable with the process of generating questions. However, when first introducing this process to the team, you may want to use one of the following lists of questions, which have been developed by team leaders and facilitators to precondition teams and encourage them to ask all the questions. Please note that the following lists were generated from businesses I have been associated with. Use them to initiate the process, and then encourage your team to come up with questions more appropriate for your particular business.

■ Questions Brainstorming Jump-Start List

Revenue

1. In what different ways can we use our facilities to generate additional revenue?

2. Are there add-on sales opportunities, where we can sell ancillary products to our existing customer base at no additional cost to us?

3. Is there value in our customer database?

4. Are there significant heavy users of our products that could be isolated into a separate group for special product offers and additional sales?

5. How often do we lose customers?

6. Can we develop a retention strategy for those customers?

7. What additional actions can we take to augment our business products or services?

8. Are there opportunities to license or franchise our business?

Salaries

1. How many hours a week do our managers work?

2. Should they be working 45 to 55 hours instead of 40?

3. How many of our employees take advantage of direct deposits for paychecks?

4. How well do we manage our salary administration program?

5. Have we established target compensation ratios based on the personality of our business?

6. Have we established a desired community position, knowing where we want to be with regard to our competition?

7. Do we have a salary administration program?

8. Do we have a salary range philosophy?

9. Do high-performing employees get higher increases than those who have not performed as well?

10. Do we establish a salary increase guideline budget and stick with it?

11. Are salary increase guidelines pre-approved?

12. Do we have a salary administration program that offers employees a salary review on an anniversary of the hire date?

13. Do we know whether our company would qualify for targeted tax job credits?

14. Do we have a training rate for all appropriate positions, where employees receive a lower rate until they are trained?

15. Do we have a 90-day probationary rate for certain positions?

16. Do we have a labor management system that helps us schedule labor in 15-minute increments?

17. Do we have a software program that reconciles cash and allows employees to cash out quickly at the end of shifts?

18. Do we constantly look for labor reductions by modifying our software?

19. Do we have industrial engineers do time-and-motion studies to determine whether additional efficiencies can be gained?

20. Do we have an incentive program to help reduce absenteeism?

21. Is our business a high-turnover business? What can be done to reduce our turnover rate?

22. Does our business utilize a vacancy factor?

23. Do we measure all of our costs by various units (such as cost per test, cost per guest check, and cost per widget) in order to determine areas of control?

Payroll Burden

1. Have we ascertained the difference between full-time and part-time employees and the benefits they should be receiving?

2. Have we evaluated the cost of our 401(k) administration program to see how competitive our costs are and to determine whether additional savings are possible?

3. Have we evaluated the cost employees are paying for participating in our benefits?

4. Have we established a vacation policy whereby vacation time must be taken the year in which it is earned?

5. Do we have a sick time buyback program whereby employees can sell back sick time at reduced rates?

6. Have we instituted a vacation buyback program allowing employees to sell back unused vacation hours at a reduced rate?

7. Have we evaluated a cafeteria-style benefits program?

8. Have we aggressively tried to reduce worker's compensation insurance by eliminating accidents?

9. Do we understand how our true burden percent is budgeted?

Communications

1. Have we authorized a telecommunications consultant to analyze our communication costs in terms of rates charged, equipment used, or programs offered? Perhaps the consultant could be compensated in accordance with a fee structure based on a percentage of the savings. If there is no savings, there is no fee.

2. How often do we renegotiate rates and terms with vendors who provide us with communication services?

Utilities

1. Have we authorized a utility consultant to analyze our utility costs?

2. Do we have in place a mandatory energy conservation program whereby thermostats are set at a standard temperature?

3. Do we have a policy that lights are turned off in conference rooms and rest rooms when these rooms are not in use?

4. Do we have a procedure for turning off all other than security lights at the close of business?

Professional Fees

1. Do we challenge fees charged by outside attorneys?

2. Have we reached an understanding about how much we will be charged, or do we just pay whatever outside professionals bill?

3. Have we sought to get the most favorable fee arrangement in each case?

4. Do we try to settle our legal cases?

5. Have outside attorneys designed a format to use for routine scenarios?

6. Have we attempted to negotiate contracts giving us a guarantee as to a minimum number of hours?

7. Do we use less expensive attorneys for small collection transactions?

8. Do we try to share costs when appropriate and make sure there are no conflicts of interest?

9. Do we give lawyers all appropriate records at the first meeting in order to eliminate the need for phone calls regarding missing items?

10. Do we insist on an itemized statement each month?

11. Do we suggest PBP approaches to the attorney? Maybe we can save the lawyer's expense, which would offset or reduce the cost of our service.

Marketing

1. Do we ensure that our advertising agency does a post-buy analysis on all advertising buys to determine whether the target rates were achieved?

2. Do we seek syndication scenarios whereby a partner would agree to fund the development of commercials and campaigns for a percentage of revenues?

3. Do we seek to have the advertising agency have some "skin in the game?"

4. Do we look for those who would partner on a percentage of the revenue?

5. Would it be possible to publish a magazine via a custom publisher and distribute it to our customer base as a way of marketing our organization and generating some additional revenue?

Public Relations

1. Should we consolidate our brochures into a few rather than have a large number of brochures?
2. Do we write our own press releases?
3. Do we seek free PR opportunities for promoting our business?
4. Do we stretch the impact of our public relations by being a good corporate citizen, sponsoring teams or working with local schools?
5. How do we rate our public relations agency? Is it getting results?
6. Is there a way to create PR events out of everyday occurrences?

Insurance

1. Are we familiar enough with our insurance policies to determine which items are covered and which are not?
2. How often do we challenge third-party providers to reduce our insurance administration costs?

Travel and Entertainment

1. Does our business need an individual who is certified as an independent travel agent so that we may receive discounts on hotel rooms, car rentals, and other travel expenses?
2. Should the company buy or lease an apartment for traveling employees rather than paying for hotel rooms?
3. Do we have a need for video conferencing? Would that solution help us reduce costs?
4. Is there a policy stating that all travel must be approved in advance and that travel authorization forms must accompany expense reports?

Facility Costs

1. Have we performed a property tax assessment comparing the cost to build a facility with the current fair market value, and have we sought adjustments when appropriate?

2. Have we ever had an accountant challenge a tax assessment?

3. How often do we evaluate our excess property? Could this property be sold or leased to reduce carrying cost?

4. Have we evaluated the sell/leaseback program?

Vehicle Costs

1. Do we have a program in place for monitoring our gasoline purchases?

2. Are our maintenance costs monitored and controlled?

3. Have we evaluated our company policy to determine whether a car allowance is better than a company-car program?

Other Supplies and Services

1. Do we need to have armored-car service, or can our managers make those deposits?

2. Have we evaluated our armored-car service to determine whether we can reduce the number of pickups?

3. Do we constantly negotiate and renegotiate prices with vendors?

4. Do we constantly renegotiate our prices with vendors to avoid the typical 3% annual inflation rate that most vendors demand?

5. Does our business recycle paper?

6. Does our business manage our trash bins to determine whether the bin sizes are appropriate? Can we get by with smaller ones or fewer pickups?

7. Have we evaluated our uniform program?

8. Are uniforms needed?

9. Should employees pick up some of the cost for the uniforms, such as cleaning expenses?

Other Expenses

1. How often do we evaluate bank charges and fees?
2. Have we evaluated the use of electronic funds transfer?
3. To how many nonprofit organizations do we contribute? Would it be better to make all contributions to a single organization?

After the facilitator introduces the jump-start questions, the team goes through the Questions Brainstorming process. Once enough questions have been generated, the facilitator leads the group through the process of prioritizing the questions and assigning responsibilities, including specific time frames for reporting back with the answers.

■ Answering the Questions

1. The PBT prioritizes the questions. This can be done in a number of ways. The team might focus on specific line items from the profit and loss statement, focus on large expense items, or choose the items most familiar to the team members. The method used depends on the company's priorities and goals.
2. The prioritized questions undergo a filtering process. Addressing each question, ask who, what, when, where, how, and why. This process builds a framework for the performance improvement planning process discussed in the next chapter.

   Example

   Question: *Do we need to have armored-car service, or can our managers make the deposits?*

   Answer: *Yes, there are organizations where managers make the deposits.*

Filter
Questions: *Who would make the deposits?*
How would it be done?
What would the activities be?
Where would the activities be done?
What bank would we use?
What procedures need to be written?
Why do we want to do this?
What type of training is needed?
When would managers do this?

3. The PBT members then take these filter questions to various individuals within the organization and research them by checking with outside sources to find the most accurate answers.

During this process, PBT members must recall the training they received on managing change throughout the organization. They should be aware of barriers to change that may exist within the organization. They must remember that some employees may even resist their asking questions about procedures. But as time goes on, the organization will become more accepting of the process and more willing to participate.

The answers to the filter questions become the information that can be turned into action items. For instance, you might assign a task force to determine how to create a procedure for managers to make deposits. The task force would determine what cost savings would be realized if this action step were put in place. Also list any additional steps necessary to accomplish this task. Determine the appropriate time frame for completing the task. Determine who is responsible for seeing the task through to completion.

■ Facilitating Questions Brainstorming

Once the Questions Brainstorming process gains momentum, the team will find it easy to come up with a long list of questions to explore. However, it is up to the manager to initiate the brainstorming process. Using the lists provided here should help. If the team is exploring an area that is unfamiliar—for example, shipping and receiving—you may want to invite a manager from that department to participate in the brainstorming session. The team will gain valuable insights, and the shipping and receiving department will become your partner in the innovation process.

A Questions Brainstorming session can also be held departmentally. A member of the Profit Building Team can act as facilitator to initiate and guide the process. The questions that are generated from this session can then be reviewed and prioritized by the PBT. This method is useful when the team needs more input from the "experts" in the area, and it encourages company-wide support of the profit building process.

■ Summary

Questions Brainstorming is a process of brainstorming questions rather than answers and solutions. This method encourages greater group participation because people are doing what comes naturally—asking questions—rather than having to come up with answers immediately.

Facilitators should use jump-start questions to stimulate a new group's thinking. As the team becomes more experienced with this process, facilitators may abandon jump-start questions.

Once enough questions have been generated, the team can begin to start seeking answers. The first step in this process is to prioritize the questions and focus on those that the team feels will have the most impact. The prioritized questions then undergo a filtering process: Examine each question by asking who, what, when, where, how, and why. Team members are assigned to research the answers further by checking with various departments and outside agencies. The answers to the filter questions are the point of departure for action items.

In the Questions Brainstorming process, the questions—and the opportunities—are endless. If you ask all the questions, you will discover that in most situations, there is more than one right answer. This process will provide you with a wealth of opportunities for cost reduction and will fuel the continuous improvement process so vital to the success of profit building. This leads us to our next step, taking action and documenting results.

7 | Taking Action and Documenting Results

Some people have ideas. A few carry them into the world of action and make them happen. These are the innovators.
—ANDREW MERCER

I have often tried to explain the synergy that takes place when a plan is constructed. Perhaps it is the chemistry of the team's collective "pull" that this commitment emphasizes, or maybe it is the psychology associated with vision, measurement, responsibility, and follow-up that leads, more times than not, to a successful conclusion.

Without falling into the trap of trying to explain why performance improvement planning works, let's just say that

Performance improvement planning works remarkably well when used as the administrative step of the Profit Building Process (PBP).

This chapter is about turning your ideas into innovations. Your performance improvement plan is the vehicle that gets you there. As you may know from your own experience, a poorly conceived plan can have you chasing after unrelated ideas without making any real progress. Taking action and documenting the results is the step of the PBP that moves you forward toward successful implementation of your ideas.

In the last chapter, we demonstrated how asking questions generates an endless list of ideas for further exploration. Our next step, taking action and documenting, shows how to use those ideas as a framework for building concrete programs for cost reduction and profit improvement.

Taking action and documenting is the performance improvement planning activity and the administrative step of the Profit Building Process. This step is essential because it helps us build and complete action steps, track results, and monitor performance, while at the same time serving as valuable program documentation.

■ The Components

Taking action and documenting can be broken down into the following components:

- Ranking PBP questions
- Formulating action steps
- Assigning responsibility
- Setting a target date
- Measuring progress
- Developing a contingency plan
- Initiating review and follow-up
- Choosing the next PBP question

It is essential to apply all of the components. Because each component builds on the previous one, skipping a step would weaken the structure of the entire process. These components, when properly applied, can lead to some powerful innovations. Here are a few examples from my own experience:

- Developing a travel policy where executives earn cash incentives for staying in hotels with room rates lower than the average rates of the previous year.
- Contracting a professional employer organization (PEO) to take over payroll and benefits administration in order to save burden cost.
- Using consultants to challenge property taxes every year in order to reap reassessment benefits.

- Finding a utility consultant to explore possible savings in past and present utility bills.

- Reviewing employee benefits programs to determine whether employees who are already receiving benefits through their spouse's health plan could forgo inclusion in the company health plan and, in return, receive higher wages.

This is just a small sample of the hundreds of innovations I have seen successfully implemented. By using effective performance improvement plans, your company will have the tools to build many further innovations of its own. Let's examine how each step of this process contributes to the performance improvement plan.

■ Ranking the Questions

The first step is ranking the questions. As we discussed in Chapter 6, PBP questions are generated during the Questions Brainstorming process. These questions are then reviewed, analyzed, and researched in order to determine whether opportunities for cost reduction exist. If so, the team ranks and prioritizes the questions. Please see Form A on the following page for an example of how to rank the questions.

Because some members may have insight into particular questions, the entire team should participate in choosing the rankings.

This simple but important step of listing and ranking questions provides the team with a valuable resource for continuous improvement. Once the top-ranking questions have been addressed, the team can move down the list to explore the other items. Remember that the Profit Building Process is full of surprises. Your team may find their greatest innovations in the lowest-ranking questions. And even rejected questions can serve as jump-start topics for the next brainstorming session.

As your team works together, it will begin to establish its own approach to ranking the questions. Here are the criteria I typically use when I look for questions:

Form A—Example

Questions—PBP

Date: _____
Team: _____

Rank	Questions
1.	Could our employees receive benefits at a lower cost?
2.	Are there ways to reduce our property taxes?
3.	How can we reduce our long-distance telephone charges?
4.	How can we reduce our legal costs?
5.	How can we reduce employee turnover?
6.	Could the company reduce costs through a job-sharing program?
7.	Could we consolidate out-of-town meetings to reduce travel costs?
8.	
9.	
10.	
11.	
12.	

- The greatest probable impact on the P&L statement
- The most enthusiasm from the team
- The lowest capital investment
- Only a minor change to a procedure or process
- A new training program as the only requirement

■ Developing a Performance Improvement Plan

Once ranked, the top questions need to be transferred to a performance improvement plan where action steps, measurement of results, and contingency planning take place. Taking the time to document these activities makes improvement planning run more smoothly, keeps the team on course, and holds individuals accountable for the success of the performance improvement plan. Using a standard form provides an easy way to measure and document the innovation process.

Take a look at Form B on the following page. Note that it is divided into eight sections: PBP Question, Action Steps, Person(s) Responsible, Target Date, Measurement, Contingency Plan (Corrective Action), Review and Follow-up, and Next PBP Question. These sections mirror the PBP components mentioned at the beginning of this chapter. We will now explore each section in more detail.

PBP Question:	In this box, record the PBP question to be addressed. Begin with the most important question—the question your team ranked number 1.
Action Steps:	This section is used to document the steps taken, the items analyzed, and the situations researched to determine whether an opportunity exists to reduce cost or improve profit. In the first meeting, you will use this box to outline basic action steps. Individuals assigned to explore these areas may also discover additional steps.

Form B—Example

Taking Action and Documenting – PBP

PBP Question	Action Steps	Persons Responsible	Target Date	Measurement	Contingency Plan	Review and Follow-up	Next PBP Question
1. Could our employees receive benefits at a lower cost?	Professional using an Employer Organization (PEO) would be appropriate and could save costs.	T. Smith M. High S. Love	2/6	Burden rate reduction of 10%	None.	PEOs are applicable. Finance and HR are assigned the responsibility to put into place.	2. Are there ways to reduce our property taxes?
PBP Question	**Action Steps**	**Person Responsible**	**Target Date**	**Measurement**	**Contingency Plan**	**Review and Follow-up**	**Next PBP Question**
2. Are there ways to reduce our property taxes?	Perform a property tax assessment, comparing cost to build with current fair market value. Hire a consultant to challenge tax assessments.	B. Reed	3/15	Annual reduction of property tax	Perform the assessment in all field locations. Have the field finance organization coordinate. Must be done by April 20.	Presentation to be made to senior management by May 1.	3. How can we reduce our long-distance telephone charges?

These can be recorded at the next meeting, when reports are given.

Action steps are the most critical part of the process. The team must make sure that the action steps they identify could lead to cost savings. Continue to challenge this process. It is another area where creativity will yield the most lucrative results.

Person(s) Responsible:

Use this box to identify those responsible for implementing the action steps. Their focus is on finding cost savings within the parameters of the PBP question.

For this position, choose someone who is creative, seeks solutions, and is able to work toward a specific target date. This person or persons will present their results to the team on a regular basis.

Target Date:

Assign a target date for completion of the action steps. Target dates are essential because they ensure that the process is driven toward completion and maintains a "living" recognition in the organization.

Target dates should not be set too far in the future or the process will lose momentum. Together, the person responsible and the team should set an agreeable target date, and the person responsible should be held to that date.

Measurement:

It is important for the team to identify how the progress of each PBP question will be measured. The measurements could be dollars/customer, dollars/employee, dollars/hour, dollars reduced per month, dollars reduced per year, and so on, as long as the focus is on cost reduction or profit improvement. The most important aspect is that the team and person(s) responsible agree on the method of measurement. All measurements should then be documented, tracked, and monitored.

Contingency Plan:

Once the process is under way, the team may discover that action steps need to be changed or that some are taking longer than anticipated. At this time, the team must meet to discuss and choose alternative approaches. Please note that when contingency plans are implemented, it is also necessary to establish new target dates.

Review and Follow-up:

As we noted earlier, the person(s) responsible for action steps must give periodic reports on their progress. Use the Review and Follow-up section of the form to record the information shared at this meeting.

At this point, one of two things will happen: Either the person responsible will report the need for a contingency plan, or, if all goes well, the action steps will result in a change or innovation that can be developed, adopted, and disseminated throughout the organization.

Next PBP Question:

In this section, write the next PBP question recorded on Form A (the list generated during Questions Brainstorming). This step emphasizes that profit building is a continuous process. There is always a next question waiting to be explored and expanded via PBP. Continue in this way through the list. When you reach the end, the team should reconvene for a review of the entire list and another questions brainstorming session. Remember that this concept is based on continuous improvement in cost reduction, which comes from analyzing an endless list of questions. As your organization gains more experience with the process, the questions will become more creative, and a higher level of profit improvement will be achieved.

■ Why Document It?

Just as Questions Brainstorming fuels profit building with endless questions to explore, the Taking Action and Documenting form (Form B) moves the process forward and supports profit building in a number of ways.

1. It enables you to organize and record the outcome of the brainstorming process.

2. It makes it easy to formulate questions into action steps with target dates, contingency plans, and responsibilities that move the process forward.

3. It supports continuous improvement, for as one question is resolved, the next is brought to the team's attention to be addressed.

It is valuable to note that "taking action and documenting" is not merely an administrative step. It is also a creative, active process. It demands the input of out-of-the-box thinkers so that the team can come up with the most effective action steps and contingency plans, and it challenges driven, committed team members to make the plans a reality. It also takes a dedicated facilitator and senior management support to keep the plan on track. As we have seen throughout this book, people are the greatest resource in the Profit Building Process.

■ Managing the Process

As team manager, you are responsible for making sure that all action steps and documentation are completed. The following tips will help you shepherd this process successfully.

Once the action steps are developed, be sure that responsibilities are clearly assigned to team members. There are a number of ways to do this: You can ask for volunteers, the team can elect someone, or you can simply assign the tasks to the team member you feel is most experienced or capable. Regardless of the method you choose, you will find that you get the best results when the team member responsible has a stake in making sure the job gets done. Perhaps the change or innovation will strongly affect this team member's department. Perhaps he or she will receive some form of compensation or is overseeing implementation of one of his or her own ideas. When the employees have a personal stake in the process, they are further motivated to get the job done.

For some employees, the simple act of being named accountable is enough to spur them on. H. James Harrington makes this point in *The Improvement Process:*

> Companies that have not been closely following the problem-correction cycle will be amazed at how long it takes to solve many of the problems. A formal system that tracks critical problems and includes the name of the individual responsible for the corrective action frequently decreases the corrective action cycle by 50 percent.[1]

Using a performance improvement planning form to assign responsibilities and set deadlines will often ensure that the action plan will be developed in a timely manner.

Occasionally, your team will run up against barriers in spite of their best efforts. This usually occurs when team members are unfamiliar with the process or department being investigated. In this case, you should support the team member in finding alternative solutions, call a team meeting for additional support or brainstorming, or assign another team member to assist in implementing the tasks. Most employees want to do a good job and will not purposely botch an assignment. By remaining supportive, you are setting an example for the team and creating a more open and trusting environment. Chastising a team member will only result in fear and distrust. And though it may appear to get you short-term results, in the long run it undermines your authority and is counterproductive.

■ Summary

Taking action and documenting is the developmental and administrative step in PBP. During this step, the team formulates and refines the performance improvement plan.

Ranking the questions, formulating action steps, assigning responsibility, setting a target date, and measuring progress are all part of this process. The forms completed at this stage also serve as documentation that will benefit future teams.

Taking action and documenting is the accelerator that propels profit building forward. This leads us to the final step, reviewing and following up—the process that (1) ensures that the proposed idea is followed through to completion and (2) initiates the next profit building cycle.

8 Reviewing Progress and Following Up

Progress has not followed a straight ascending line, but a spiral with rhythms of progress and regression, of evolution and dissolution.
—GOETHE

As stated throughout this book, PBP is a dynamic, continuous process. Its management concepts, when systematically applied, result in continuity of profit improvement and cost reduction. Reviewing and following up is the essential last step that keeps the process going. Its critical role is to create a perpetual improvement process, while keeping innovations current with today's business needs and ensuring longevity.

In many organizations, management has the habit of dropping a change or innovation from its agenda once the action steps are under way. Managers are so sure of their success and so eager to move on to the next item that they forget to follow up on their latest innovation. Consequently, the organization forgets, too, and the innovation fails.

Other management teams adopt the opposite approach. They work so hard on developing a change or innovation that they can't let go. They try to force it through the organization, ignoring any feedback that suggests the action steps they developed no longer apply. Once again, the innovation is doomed.

Reviewing and following up is the step that can help your organization avoid these two pitfalls. By applying three basic concepts, your team will learn to inspect, evaluate, and monitor innovations and action steps while perpetuating the PBP process. Reviewing and following up includes

1. A comprehensive review of each action step to determine whether the cost-saving idea or solution has merit and can be adopted by the organization.

2. A timely follow-up to ensure that the person responsible is in fact taking the necessary steps to complete the assignments generated via the performance improvement plan.

3. A spark of ignition, forcing the team to ask the perpetual question "What is the next PBP question?"

This chapter will examine each of these three areas. But first, I would like to illustrate the value of reviewing and following up with an example from my own experience.

■ My Learning Experience

During the early 1980s, I learned firsthand how vital reviewing and following up is to performance improvement planning. I was responsible for an operations plan that was moving into the fourth quarter. I was challenged by my supervisor to find a way for the organization to achieve a higher level of profit contribution than our current trends were indicating. This was not a new request, nor was my approach a new one. I quickly organized my team, and we put together a plan that I felt was realistic and would get the job done.

Shortly after the plan was submitted and approved, we started our financial planning for the next year. Our starting point was the projections that were approved in our performance improvement plan.

Unfortunately, there was a problem. Although I did follow-up the first month or two to see whether my performance improvement plan was working, I failed to continue to track its progress. The plan started well, but performance dropped off, and my team did not react in time to correct this slump and meet the planned goals. Assuming that we were on track to achieve our stated results, I gave directions to use a more aggressive year-end target.

Needless to say, this mistake not only affected our performance in the last quarter of the current year but also caused us problems with the first quarter of the next year. This learning experience, though painful at the time, drove home the need for constant review. I will never again miss my projections because of failure to follow up! I learned the hard way that this step is crucial to successful idea implementation. It is the final, crucial step of the Profit Building Process.

■ A Thorough Inspection

Because organizations have many complex aspects that may be philosophical, that may be strategic, or that may even raise legal questions, it is important to inspect and examine each action step before implementing it throughout the organization. The process of reviewing and following up allows for a timely retrospective on action items as well as an opportunity for criticism and/or correction. It is important that each idea be researched prior to implementation. State laws may be relevant. What works in some states may not be appropriate in others. Take time to reexamine each action step and determine whether it is still "to code"—that is, effective and appropriate for the organization.

Over time, changes occurring in the organization may make the innovation obsolete. Robert Fritz emphasizes this point in *Corporate Tides: The Inescapable Laws of Corporate Structure.*

> Current reality changes as we do our work. Current reality is not the situation that existed the last time we happened to look. It needs to be continually updated. As we complete action steps, their accomplishments need to be listed . . . .
> Perhaps we need to include new action steps to address

these changes in reality. As we execute action plans, we make mistakes. How do we learn from those mistakes? Some of this information will need to appear in updates of current reality and adjustments to our action plans.[1]

The fast-changing business environment makes review essential. The action steps that are created today may be outdated by tomorrow. To remain effective, innovations and action steps must be carefully reviewed.

The profit building team should take as much time in evaluating and critiquing each action step as it did when it first explored cost-saving ideas. A thorough critique will not only provide some reassurance that cost-saving opportunities still exist; it will also give the team a second chance to support this particular innovation as one they want to recommend for adoption and later diffusion.

Once a particular action step has been developed, a follow-up assessment—especially with the possibility of change—adds value to all ideas that pass this reassessment. Team members gain confidence as the innovation clears each hurdle. Careful review also gives the team the opportunity to reject an action step or innovation as unlikely to succeed. This saves the entire organization the effort and frustration of trying to implement an innovation that simply will not work.

In addition, the comprehensive review provides the evaluation necessary to document the potential results of the idea. Please remember that it is the team's perceived results that set the performance goals. The team is holding itself accountable for devising effective cost reduction and action steps, one at a time.

■ Timely Follow-up

Once the team has reviewed each action step of the proposed innovation, a date should be set for following up on the results. During the follow-up meeting, the person responsible for taking charge of the action steps reports on the progress that he/she has made. The action steps may include research, design, meeting with other departments, or finding a consultant. This formal means of monitoring progress increases the team's effectiveness by holding individuals accountable to meet their commitments; it ensures that the project will be seen through to completion. It also gives the team the opportunity to provide input on contingency plans or corrective action steps, if needed. All teams must develop this process in order to achieve results.

Timely follow-up is the finishing piece that delivers the end result. Therefore, managers have to maintain the energy of the process by pursuing the performance improvement plan and motivating the team to make sure that no stones are left unturned in the quest for profit improvement. In a recent interview in *Fast Company*, Peter Senge outlines some basic yet effective motivational factors that would apply here.

> There are a number of self-reinforcing factors that help a pilot program take root. People develop a personal stake in it. People see that their colleagues take it seriously, and they want to be part of a network of committed people. There's also a pragmatic factor: It works. There are real business results—so it's worthwhile to become engaged. But the most fundamental reinforcement of a pilot program is hearing people say that they've found a better way of working. Most people would rather work with a group of people who trust one another. Most people would rather walk out of a meeting with the belief that they've just solved an important problem. Most people would rather have fun at work. It may seem obvious, but what we've observed again and again is that personal enthusiasm is the initial energizer of any change process. And that enthusiasm feeds on itself. [2]

As manager, you will find that your enthusiasm and belief in the PBP process and its resulting innovations are necessary to keep your team excited and committed. This is vital to your team's success. PBP can slow to a stop if management is not effective in the follow-up stage. The team could stop meeting, stop preparing itself for adopting innovations, or run out of creative questions to evaluate. Follow-up is the process in which the team reinforces and establishes previous action by continuing to review, monitor, and provide both positive and negative feedback to keep the process going.

The entire organization should also be made aware of the status of the innovation and action steps being reviewed. This can be achieved through memos, meetings, or newsletters. Management may also find it valuable to create a forum for employee feedback, such as a survey or suggestion box used explicitly for input on a particular innovation and its action steps. This keeps innovation in the forefront throughout the organization, eventually making it a part of the company culture.

■ Igniting the Process

Once reviewing and following up is completed, the team moves the innovation along for adoption and diffusion. The results can be recorded on the Reviewing and Following Up form (Form C). This form allows you to record the PBP question, a short analysis of the situation, and the amount of profit improvement. The Reviewing and Following Up form serves as a record of your team's performance and provides documentation for future teams.

Take a look at the Situation Analysis column on the form. This is the place to record the status of the innovation, the amount of cost savings achieved, any ongoing steps, processes that have been put on hold, and so on. For accurate tracking, be sure to date your notes and attach any necessary back-up documentation.

Occasionally, a PBP question will reveal the need for a project that is so large that it is more than the team can handle effectively on its own. This type of project is best handled by a separate project management team, with its own timeline and detailed profit improvement plan. The PBT should monitor the project to make sure that all steps are completed and should continue to track the results on the Reviewing and Following Up form.

Form C—Example

Reviewing and Following Up—PBP

PBP Question	Situation Analysis	Profitability Improvement
1. Could our employees receive benefits at a lower cost?	A PEO was contacted and determined the organization can save 10% on burden cost.	Improvement to date is $100,000
2. Are there ways to reduce property taxes?	Assessments are taking place across the country. Five programs completed.	As of 3/30: $75,000 saved
3.		
4.		
5.		
6.		
7.		
8.		
9.		

■ Asking the Next PBP Question

When the process is complete and results have been recorded, it is time to ask, "What is the next PBP question?" The simple process of asking this question reignites the Profit Building Process and returns it to the beginning; exploring the next question from the brainstorming list.

Asking the next PBP question is such a critical step that I recommend emphasizing it throughout the organization. "What is the next PBP question?" should become a theme for department meetings. It should be brought up with consultants, discussed during interviews with outside candidates, and mentioned in probationary reviews and performance reviews.

When the organization reaches the level of execution where every employee is asking, "What is the next PBP question?" it has arrived at the point all companies should seek: continuous implementation of cost reduction and profit improvement.

As a profit building manager, you are responsible for creating enthusiasm and interest in PBP. Your team, and perhaps the entire organization, will be looking to you for leadership and reassurance that their efforts are generating results.

Here are some suggestions for keeping PBP going:

- Learn from your mistakes. Make it clear to your team that some of the questions will not make it all the way through the performance improvement plan to implementation. As an idea is explored more deeply, it may become apparent that it simply will not work. Some team members may see this as a failure and become frustrated with the process, especially if they had a personal stake in that particular question or innovation. It is helpful to frame unsuccessful innovations in a positive light by pointing out what the team learned from the experience and stressing that the decision to drop the proposed innovation was an intelligent one. After all, an issue that warranted attention was addressed, and a potential profit building idea was explored.

- Post your successes. In your conference room and in team members' offices, post successful innovations, including the amount of money they have saved. You may also want to post them throughout the organization or to list them on a memo sent out periodically to all departments. Posting your successes serves as a reminder of the achievements of the profit building team and keeps the focus on profitability improvement.

- Celebrate your successes. Every time the team successfully develops a question into a means of cost reduction, hold a group celebration. It could be as simple as a team lunch or dinner—whatever works for your team. When the entire organization incorporates a particularly successful money-saving innovation, a company-wide celebration, such as a company picnic, may be appropriate. The point is to recognize the team's accomplishments and its contribution to the organization through PBP.

One celebration that stands out in my mind took place while I was president of a national auto glass company. The results my team achieved were a real stretch for everyone involved. We would not have been successful if it weren't for everyone pulling his and her own weight, and then some. To celebrate, we developed a self-funding pool of money for recognizing employees' achievements. We decided to host a dinner cruise, complete with music, a talent show, and awards for individual achievements.

The feeling of excitement, morale, and confidence that surrounded this event was so great that we continued to use this incentive each quarter to keep employees focused on current targets. Together we created an organization that knew how to achieve results, and our celebration of success became the motivator that kept it going.

■ The Manager's Role in Implementing the Innovation

After exploring the action steps, the team will determine whether the innovation is appropriate and should be implemented. During this process, the team manager must guide the team in reaching a decision that is agreeable to all. Those who have a personal stake in the innovation or have donated a lot of time to its development may try to push the innovation through to completion. The manager must keep the atmosphere open to contingency plans and feedback.

During the reviewing and following-up stage, it is important to continue to seek feedback from the employees who will be most affected by the innovation or change. I recommend that you set up periodic meetings with department managers to follow up on the progress being made. This is also a good time to discuss any needed adjustments or corrective action steps that will make the process run smoother.

Real change will not occur without the support and teamwork of the entire organization. As the team manager, it is your responsibility to drum up excitement continually and elicit further cost-saving ideas. Offer incentives, celebrations, and awards. Keep up the momentum and you will see successful idea implementation and the resulting profit improvements. Senior management can also play a role if the process slows. You must recognize this need if it arises and react when appropriate.

■ Summary

The final step in the process, reviewing and following up, keeps the PBP moving forward. This step ensures that the proposed innovation is followed through to completion; then it starts the Profit Building Process all over again. Reviewing and following up consists of three steps: comprehensive review, timely follow up, and the "ignition process" of asking the next question.

A comprehensive review of each action step will determine whether the cost-saving idea has merit and can be adopted and diffused throughout the organization. Timely follow-up ensures that action steps are being completed and gives the team the opportunity to provide further input or take corrective measures. The final element, asking the next PBP question, ignites and restarts the Profit Building Process, emphasizing the fact that it is a perpetual cycle.

As the organization becomes more familiar with the Profit Building Process and its results, they will come to depend on it as a valuable profit improvement and cost reduction tool. Employees will have cost reduction in the back of their minds as they complete their tasks and will gradually become aware of more and more ways to save. Over time, the Profit Building Process will become a core competency of the organization.

The next two chapters will give you more than 100 ideas for cost reduction and profit improvement. Evaluate these lists to determine whether some of these ideas are right for *your* organization.

9 | Fifty Action Steps for Immediate Profit Improvement

Various fresh ideas gained acceptance . . . when they could be presented not as something radically new, but as the revival in modern terms of a time-honored principle or practice that had been forgotten.
—B. H. LIDDELL HART

Creativity will usually find a home in the more innovative aspects of business. In most companies, activities like marketing new products, locating retail sites, and building out facilities are zealously attacked with a barrage of inventive action plans. But when it comes to cost cutting and profit improvement, a lack of ingenuity, a dull, mindless repetition of what was done before often prevails. Yet, as I have stated throughout this book, profitability is one of the main purposes of business and should be approached with the same creative energy and enthusiasm as the more tangible aspects of business. As you will discover for yourself, a little ingenuity can lead to big savings and profit improvement.

One of the best examples of the need for applying creative thinking to cost reduction came up while I was Senior Vice President of Operations for an automotive emissions testing business. Our business consisted of fourteen individual state programs, each independently negotiated via a seven-to-ten year contract. These contracts gave us the right to test vehicle emissions to determine whether they met EPA standards in that state. In a typical year, we tested approximately 15 million vehicles.

Because each contract was individually negotiated, we thought it appropriate to evaluate each state program based on the typical "budget vs. actual" concept. If a program were on budget, we would move to the next program without further analyzing the situation.

We thought this approach was sufficient. However, during one of our profit-building sessions, a team member came up with an idea that opened up new avenues for additional substantial savings. The idea was simple: for every program, divide each P&L cost item by the number of vehicles tested. Then, use this cost-per-test calculation to compare each program and chart the results.

Once in use, this process gave us a very different view of profitability. Programs that looked good on a cash-flow basis showed opportunities for improvement when measured via cost-per-test and compared to similar programs with like equipment and test procedures. After examining these results, we identified several areas of concern and developed action plans.

One line item's results varied so widely from program to program that it called for further investigation. This was "other personnel cost per test," and consisted of benefits cost, vacation cost, workers compensation, and other employee-related expenses. By asking further questions, we discovered that workers' compensation costs deviated significantly from one program to the next. Once we identified the problem, our team developed the following action steps. Our excellent human resources director quickly put these steps into place:

- *We held a problem-solving meeting with our insurance carrier and challenged their safety engineers, claims processing personnel, and administrative team to develop training and accident prevention ideas.*
- *An accident prevention committee was put into place at each testing station. These committees were responsible for reducing the number of accidents month by month.*

- *Each action prevention committee held a monthly meeting. Minutes from the meeting were sent to the corporate human resources office.*

- *To increase injury prevention, we developed a station house-keeping procedure, establishing an attitude of a place for everything and everything in its place.*

- *We stressed the use of proper safety equipment (safety glasses, earplugs, and other equipment). At one station, faulty equipment was identified as a source of accidents and was promptly replaced.*

- *A monthly safety communication was sent to all stations. The communication reinforced a "safety first" policy and reviewed safety procedures.*

- *4,000 employees were retrained on safety in the workplace.*

- *We created several new positions specifically designed for employees who were injured on the job. These positions allowed employees to return to work earlier than was expected.*

- *Safety engineers were contracted for the sole purpose of making recommendations for improving the safety of equipment and procedures.*

These and other creative action steps reduced our workers' compensation costs by nearly $1 million dollars in a single year. One small creative idea, a simple change in the way we measured results, led us to uncover new problem areas with potential savings that were previously hidden.

Think of the questions that go unasked every day and the potential savings that are never unearthed in your organization, because creative thinking is not applied to profit improvement. Clearly, creative thinking and brainstorming does have a place in cost reduction and profit improvement plans, and is, in fact, the backbone of the PBP. The list of ideas included in this chapter were generated through the creative Questions Brainstorming process. And although this book provides more than a hundred cost-cutting ideas encompassing a wide range of departments, it is just the beginning. The ideas your team can come up with are endless.

■ How to Use the List

In this chapter and in the next, you'll find a list of specific cost-cutting and profit-improvement ideas to help you get started on your own profit improvement plans. These ideas were generated by various teams using PBP and have been used by other companies with great success. I suggest you start by doing the following:

- Read through the list in order to identify those item(s) that have the potential to reduce cost or improve the profitability of your business or organization.

- Review selected items with your finance department, human resources department, and your legal department.

- Allow your PBT to review the list to determine potential use.

- During Questions Brainstorming, use the list to stimulate additional ideas that may be more appropriate for your business. Make sure that any ideas you try are appropriate for your company.

I include this list for several reasons: the ideas can be applied immediately to initiate profit improvement; the ideas can be used to jump-start the brainstorming process; and perhaps most importantly, the list demonstrates the type of effective solutions that team specifically designed for cost reduction can produce.

As you read through the list and present it to your team, the wide range of ideas that are generated through this process may strike you. As this list illustrates, all areas of the P&L statement present opportunities for cost reduction. It is my intention that this list of ideas will encourage your team to go beyond traditional action steps and encourage more creative solutions, so that all possible avenues will be explored.

Finally, the list in this chapter concentrates on revenue enhancement, salaries, and other personnel costs. Unlike lists you may have found in other management books, this one was developed using a process designed to continuously reduce costs and improve profits by both individuals and specifically customized teams. Cost reduction is a continuous process, and management should constantly have a source of ideas that, if applied, would make the business more profitable. Using the Profit Building Process, your company can construct additional thoughts and solutions. Follow the steps we have discussed and your organization will be on the way to lowering costs and raising levels of profitability. It is hoped that this list will also provide some viable alternatives to layoffs.

■ Ideas to Reduce Costs and Build Profits

Category	Idea Numbers
Revenue	1–10
Salaries	11–35
Other Personnel Costs	36–50

■ Revenue

Snapshot

This category typically contains in-flows of resources (assets) into the business generated through operations.

Needless to say, the Profit Building Process can be used to generate marketing and sales ideas. The following ideas were generated with the objective of increasing revenue with *little or no impact on the cost structure*.

Cost-Saving Ideas

1. If your company has facilities located over a multi-geographical territory, you may be able to rent "antenna space" to cellular phone companies. Typically, these companies will pay for the use of rooftops as a place to erect their antennas. This enhances your revenue without any additional cost to you.

   Comment: The point here is to explore alternative uses for your facilities. Remember that they are assets that can be used 24 hours a day, 7 days a week. There are numerous opportunities available for increased revenue if you look for them.

2. Determine whether your business can market commission or non-commission products as "add-on" sales.

   Comment: Look for opportunities to sell products to your existing customer base at no additional cost. We all know examples of this, such as catalog sales to airline passengers and the sale of miscellaneous products to credit card customers. You may have the opportunity to do something similar. Your customers have more value than you realize.

3. Is there additional value in your customer database? Perhaps your business could generate additional revenue by selling the data. Alternatively, consider starting a telemarketing department to market another line of products or services.

   Comment: Depending on your business and the nature of your customer base, you may have something big here!

4. Explore the advantages of an effective e-strategy, including e-commerce, e-business, e-people, and e-technology.

   Comment: There is no question that the new opportunities available through the Internet offer new and innovative ways to increase profits and reduce costs. Consult with an expert in this area (including a cross section of employees) and magic will happen!

5. Segment your customers into "heavy user" and "light user" categories to determine the difference between these two groups. What needs to be done to generate another sale or occasion from both categories?

   Comment: All customers are critical. What can you learn about the different types of customers to determine whether more occasions are possible? Make the most of these customers—you already have them!

6. Develop retention strategies as well as growth strategies. In today's markets, it is as important to hold on to your existing customer base as it is to grow your business.

   Comment: It took you a certain amount of resources to attract your customers: You may want to explore ways to retain a higher percentage. What is your cost to acquire a customer? What is your cost to retain a customer? Do your employees know?

7. Continue to look for augmentative businesses, products, and/or services that would add value without adding expense.

8. Explore opportunities to license or franchise your business products or services for additional market share or penetration.

9. Explore merger and acquisition scenarios where efficiencies could be gained for all businesses concerned.

10. Develop a relationship with a long-distance carrier whereby your company will distribute phone cards to your customer base in return for a fee or residual commission.

■ Salaries

Snapshot

This category typically contains charges associated with (a) management pay, (b) non-management pay, (c) hourly wages, (d) training labor, (e) overtime pay, and (f) all other pay, wages, and salary items.

Cost-Saving Ideas

11. Establish a 45- to 60-hour per-week work environment among managers. Cost structures among your competitors are basically similar to your cost structure, so you will obtain an advantage because your managers are working more hours. (This assumes that your managers are productive.)

    Comment: I know what you're thinking—management would never accept such a policy. But consider this: Managers who have responsibility for a workforce of hourly employees are usually at the facility, retail outlet, restaurant, or office at least this amount of time. Sometimes business volume is extremely low at early or closing hours. During these light hours, managers can save substantially by scheduling fewer employees and filling in themselves. In addition to the labor savings, managers will become more knowledgeable about operations and will find ways to improve customer service, training, and operations.

    I have put this procedure in place several times. At the beginning there will always be resistance, but once managers get beyond the initial "hump," things will run smoothly.

    I also find that certain incentive programs work well here. Give the managers incentives based on labor dollars saved, and they come to understand the process.

12. Encourage all employees to take advantage of direct deposit for their paychecks. This reduces the cost of generating paychecks. Hold contests or offer small incentives to build acceptance of direct deposit.

13. Effectively manage your salary administration programs. Many companies pay "lip service" to this principle but fail to obtain true levels of success in salary administration management. To start, make sure you have a salary range for every position in the company. Salaries should be structured so that the midpoint is 100%, the minimum is 80%, and the maximum is 120%.

The basic philosophy is that a candidate should be hired into a position between the minimum (80% range) and the midpoint (100% range) on the basis of his or her level of experience. The employee is then moved higher in the range on the basis of performance. This philosophy is based on the premise that midpoint (100% of range) is the amount the position is worth to the company. An employee can still obtain an additional 20% through stellar performance. Few employees should be paid over 120% of range.

Comment: Each job is worth a specific amount to the organization. If a new hire needs training to become efficient in a particular job, that employee is working at a level below the "worth" of the position and therefore should be paid at the minimum of the salary range. When the employee's performance rises to successful completion of 100% of the job duties, move the employee quickly toward the midpoint of the salary range.

14. Establish a target compensation ratio based on the personality of your business. Compensation ratio is the average position in the salary range by job classification. If your business is a high-turnover business, an 85% target may be reasonable. A low-turnover business may have a target close to 100% compensation ratio. This type of measurement will let you know whether your company is overpaying for various positions, and whether you are moving employees too quickly through the salary range.

Comment: Again, for a salary range:

80%	**85%**	100%	120%
	_____	_____	_____	
Minimum	***Target***	*Midpoint*	*Maximum*

Some industries have high turnover for normal business reasons. Typical examples of this situation are retail and restaurant operations. These businesses employ a part-time workforce. Because of the nature of the business, most employees are usually hired at the minimum of the salary range and usually leave before reaching midpoint. Therefore, the average compensation ratio should be managed below midpoint. The 85% target represents this scenario.

Most organizations do not manage their labor this way. Have your human resources department perform this analysis and make a presentation based on the results. I am confident that you will find opportunities for more management in this area.

15. Insist that a salary survey be done every year to ensure that you have achieved the desired community position (DCP) relative to your competition. In this case, the competition is those companies that would recruit your employees. You need to make sure that if you survey 10 competitors, you have salary ranges higher than 75% of these companies for your key positions and higher than 50% of these companies for lower-level positions. Implementing this strategy will help you reduce turnover and will also ensure that you are not overpaying for positions.

16. Make sure your salary administration program allows for a regular salary review. Typically, this is done once a year for salaried employees and every six months for hourly employees. The review should include a performance appraisal form where employees' performance levels correspond with established pay increases. In other words, establish a "pay for performance" review system.

17. Establish a bell curve for salary increases. Let's say that approximately 8% of your employees are superior performers, 12% are above average, 60% are average, 12% are fair, and 8% are poor. Create a salary increase guideline that mirrors this curve, with the better-performing employees receiving higher increases. For example, superior employees are given 6% to 7%, above-average employees 4% to 5%, average employees 3%, fair employees 2%, and poor

employees 0%. This allows the organization to reward its top performers while still meeting its salary increase budget.

Comment: Obviously, your goal is to continue to train and develop your workforce. Occasionally, low-performing or inappropriate employees have to be replaced with those more suited to the position. The bell curve is just a process to ensure that star performers are recognized and rewarded for their work.

18. Establish the salary increase guideline budget and stick to it. Plan salary increases for the coming year by using the bell curve mentioned in idea 17. Department managers should plan salary increases for employees by assuming that next year's performance will be at the same level as this year's.

    Comment: Please be aware that some performance ratings will change. There will always be exceptions. This process will help ensure that your organization will remain within your salary increase budget.

19. The salary increase guidelines budget should be preapproved. When a different rating is submitted during the year, treat it as an exception and make sure it is justified because performance can change—it may go up or down. A strict salary administration program will ensure that budgets are achieved.

20. If you have a salary increase administration program that offers employees a salary review based on an anniversary date or hire date, this means your organization is administrating salary throughout the year. At the end of the fiscal year, why not consider moving the organization to a "focal review," a date when the entire organization is reviewed at the same time? This would allow for better administration and control and, more important, a substantial one-year savings on your labor cost.

Example

Assume that your company is on an October 2000–September 2001 fiscal year. Your organization makes an announcement on August 1, 2000 that starting in fiscal year 2001, there will be a focal review on April 15, 2001. These reviews will be based on performance, with top performers achieving 7% increases and poor performers achieving 0% increases. The normal review cycle would take place for the remainder of fiscal year 2000. Also assume that this organization has planned a 3% salary increase guideline for fiscal year 2001.

No salary increase is given from 10/1/2000 through 4/14/2001. Therefore, there is no salary increase impact on your labor cost for the first six months of fiscal year 2001.

On April 15, 2001, every employee would receive a 0% to 7% increase, which would be managed to deliver a 3% annual impact on labor cost. Please note that this 3% impact would affect only six months of fiscal year 2001. In other words, the annual impact of the 3% planned salary increase guidelines would only be 1.5% because of the salary administration change and the fact that no increases were given from 10/1/2000 to 4/15/2001.

It is important to note that this is a one-time positive impact. The next year would demonstrate the 3% impact for the entire year. But depending on the size of your organization, a one-time 1.5% positive hit to labor could be significant.

Comment: It may sound extreme, but when faced with the alternative of laying off employees, this is a good idea. Cost is saved and jobs are saved. Open and honest communication is crucial here. Don't try to trick or fool your organization. You will win their support once they realize the reason behind the policy. This one-time positive impact may be all you need to make it through a difficult year.

21. Establish a training rate for all appropriate positions. This is crucial when your organization experiences higher levels of turnover during the first and second months of employment. The training rate is lower than the standard pay rate and is applicable only during the training period. Employees are given a raise once the training has been completed satisfactorily. Determine whether a training rate could be established for all positions in the organization.

22. Where a training rate is not appropriate, establish a probationary rate for the standard 90-day period. This rate is lower than the standard pay rate and is applicable only during the first 90 days of employment. If performance is satisfactory, the employee will receive a raise to the standard pay rate. Determine whether a probationary rate could be established for all positions in the organization.

23. Develop a labor management system (LMS) whereby a computer predicts daily or hourly volume and the amount of labor needed on the basis of seasonality. Most businesses have a trend or cycle that can be measured with 15-minute increments. First, you must get past the notion that your business cannot be tracked this way. There *is* a pattern to your business. Discovering your business pattern is the first step toward determining how to manage your labor cost.

    Comment: Management will give you many reasons why the business cannot be tracked. Once you work through all of their concerns, you and your team can identify those core items, trends, or aspects of your customer behavior that, in fact, can be tracked and schedule labor accordingly.

24. Determine whether your new hires would qualify for the Targeted Job Tax Credit (TJTC) program whereby a percentage of training dollars is refunded.

25. Determine whether your organization would qualify for tax benefits for providing employee child care services.

26. If your employees handle cash transactions, install a software-driven cash reconciliation process to save time at shift changes and at closing. This will also reduce cash shortages.

    Comment: This type of procedure also saves time in the cash-out process.

27. Constantly look for software modifications that can reduce labor. Seconds saved could mean dollars earned.

    Comment: Using technology is a natural approach to the whole effort of productivity improvement. If your business has not recently explored this area, the effective tools that currently exist may surprise you.

28. Have an industrial engineer evaluate your business in terms of time and motion studies to determine whether additional efficiencies can be achieved in areas where high throughput is important.

    Comment: This approach can still work today. Some managers run their businesses the same way they did 10 or 20 years ago. Time and motion studies can have an impact on cost savings, productivity, customer service, and employee morale.

29. Establish a self-regulating team with the specific responsibility of improving productivity and reducing cost in a particular department or area of the organization.

30. Develop an incentive to reduce absenteeism. This incentive should be linked to productivity improvement goals and to the availability of the workforce. It should be based on reduced absenteeism from a previous period. The incentive could be a vacation bonus based on a 1% reduction in absenteeism.

31. Set up a policy stating that management will randomly call or visit sick employees. Employees need to understand the clear relationship between reducing absenteeism and improving productivity.

    Comment: Most managers and employees know when particular co-workers are taking advantage of sick leave.

Making random calls will reduce absenteeism. Remember that the PBP approach includes examining all areas of the business where an improvement can save cost and prevent layoffs.

32. Develop a variable pay program whereby management salaries are reduced 5% to 10% across the board, and these dollars are set aside into a bonus pool. Through goal achievement, managers have the potential to earn even higher levels of compensation. However, these dollars will be at risk if managers do not achieve profit objectives.

    Comment: The potential to earn even higher levels of compensation will help sell this item.

33. If your business is a high-turnover business for hourly employees and management, plan a vacancy factor. A vacancy factor is a percentage factor applied to that period of time from when an employee terminates employment to when he or she is replaced on the payroll. Most business plans assume that a certain number of employees will be in position for a full year. Every time a turnover occurs and an hour, a day or a week goes by without a replacement, there is positive P&L impact. By applying a vacancy factor, management can present a more profitable plan based on reality. A conservative rule of thumb is to reduce your labor cost in accordance with the following table:

Turnover Rate	Labor Cost Reduction
80%–100%	1%
100%–150%	2%
150% and up	3%

After your labor plan is developed, reduce it by the percentage above that corresponds to historical turnover rates.

Comment: You may be surprised to learn how high employee turnover is in certain industries. If your industry experiences high turnover, understanding the true P&L impact will help you develop more accurate plans.

34. Controlling your turnover is another way to reduce operating cost. Implement procedures throughout the entire human resources cycle to ensure that all systems, procedures, policies, and practices are airtight, preventing employees from falling through the cracks.

    Comment: I refer to this as the human resources "closed loop." If you think about it, you will see that there is a cycle to the human resources process. It starts with recruitment, interviewing, selection, and placement and continues through orientation, training, salary administration, performance appraisal, development, promotion, and finally, termination. Then the cycle begins again. Make sure that all of the areas mentioned are "employee-friendly" and are designed to retain employees. Identify any areas wherein improvements would reduce the number of employees leaving.

35. In order to determine where to place additional controls, measure your labor costs in terms of cost per unit, cost per test, cost per guest check, etc.

    Comment: Breaking your labor costs down to the lowest unit will help you better identify cost-saving ideas. It will also make them easier to affect and control.

■ Other Personnel Costs

> ### Snapshot
>
> This category would typically contain charges associated with (a) applied payroll burden, (b) FICA—employer's portion, (c) FUTA, (d) vacation, (e) paid holidays, (f) sick leave, (g) bonuses, (h) SUI, (I) 401(k) employer's matching, (j) short-/long-term disability, (k) group medical, etc.

Cost-Saving Ideas

36. Make sure your company has a program that offers all full-time employees the opportunity to receive a higher salary in lieu of accepting certain benefits (such as medical, dental, and life insurance). Today, many employees are being carried on a spouse's plan. Why not let those employees choose a higher salary instead of benefits? As long as the salary increase is less than the cost of benefits, the company will save money and the employees will increase their income.

37. Evaluate the cost of your 401(k) administration. There are competitive programs that can reduce administrative costs.

    Comment: A simple evaluation by three different companies will determine whether you have an opportunity to realize savings.

38. Evaluate the dollar amount employees are paying for participating in the benefits program. Could employees cover a higher percentage of this cost?

    Comment: Again, keep in mind that these are cost reduction ideas for preventing layoffs. In this environment, tough business decisions have to be made. First evaluate the situation, and then choose your approach. You may decide to split the savings with the employees by turning half of the impact back into compensation.

39. Establish a vacation policy whereby vacation time is taken the year it is earned. It is costly to pay out vacations at the current salary at the time the vacation is taken, even though the vacation may have been earned a year or more ago at a lower wage.

    Comment: This policy will help control productivity, administrative fees and scheduling and will actually save costs because it ensures that employees are paid vacation pay at the salary rate in place the year it was earned.

40. Institute a vacation and sick time buyback program whereby employees can sell back sick time at a reduced rate.

Comment: There are times when this works well for all parties concerned.

41. Evaluate your organization to determine whether using a professional employer organization (PEO) could be beneficial. A PEO contractually assumes and manages critical human resources and personnel responsibilities and employer risks by establishing and maintaining an employer relationship with work site employees. Because of this relationship, hiring, payroll, salary administration, benefits, payroll tax, recruiting, and employee relations are all handled by the PEO at a cost negotiated to be less than what the employer is spending today.

    Comment: This approach can be a tremendous benefit to your business. It could also be beneficial for your employees. Better benefits plans may also evolve. Best Staff Services, Inc. in Houston, Texas, is an example of a PEO.

42. Install a cafeteria-style benefits program whereby employees can choose the benefits they want rather than accepting a standard package.

43. Reduce worker's compensation insurance by aggressively reducing accidents. Evaluate your worker's compensation accrual to determine your claims history. Most companies set an accrual rate and never reevaluate it even though their experience changes.

    Comment: Depending on your business, you may be surprised at the potential savings here.

44. Understand your true burden percentage and budget it. Challenge your finance and human resources departments to give you accurate numbers so that you can budget the actual percentage rather than an approximation. The P&L should reflect the actual burden percentage and not an estimate that was set at the start of the year and never changed.

45. Using the Internet, conduct benefits surveys to compare your costs with those of similar organizations.

46. Challenge third-party providers to reduce their administration costs by using the PBP—and passing those savings along to you!

47. Continue to monitor worker's compensation costs and develop action plans to reduce them.

48. Develop a "back-to-work" program that puts injured employees in alternative positions. There are times when injured employees want to remain active in the organization and appropriate positions are available.

49. Negotiate settlements when long-term worker's compensation situations dictate.

50. Eliminate alcohol at all company-sponsored activities.

    Comment: This approach can prevent accidents, cut beverage costs at functions, and reduce risks.

■ Summary

We have just taken a look at some of the cost-saving opportunities available in the following categories: revenue, salaries, and payroll burden (other personnel costs). Work with these ideas and tailor them to your organization's specific needs or use them as a starting point for your team's brainstorming sessions. Remember that these are just a small sampling of the many ideas that can be generated through PBP. We will explore additional profit building ideas for communications, utilities, professional fees, marketing, and public relations in the next chapter.

10 Sixty Further Steps to Cut Costs in All Areas of Your Business

The stock of ideas which mankind has to work with is very limited, like the alphabet, and can at best have an air of freshness given it by new arrangements and combinations, or by application to new times and circumstances.
—JAMES RUSSELL LOWELL

In most businesses, reviewing expenses as a percentage of revenue reveals that salaries and other personnel costs equate to 20%–45% of the P&L. Because of this, these areas are typically the first to be examined in the search for lower costs.

Though this is a common and effective first step, we can still take cost-cutting further and reap even greater results. I like to ask my teams the following question:

"If labor-related costs are 40%, by all means let's analyze! However, what about the remaining 60%? Doesn't it seem likely that we have additional opportunities within these other line items?"

This chapter will address cost-cutting approaches to this remaining 60%—those areas that are waiting to be discovered but are often ignored.

The need for uncovering these hidden profits became apparent to me during an extended business trip in 1997. I was fortunate to be one of three executives who helped to sell our corporation via a strategic initiative in the capital market. The process was the most challenging that I have been a part of to-date in my career. We stayed at the Grand Hyatt New York for about three months until the transaction was complete.

It was during this time that I first began to consider writing this book. We presented for numerous hours to arguably some of the best deal-makers on Wall Street. Yet they continued to probe deeper, searching for some silver bullet to account for our dramatic cash-flow improvement that occurred in just over a two-year period. It was then that I realized that Profit Building is a unique process. There was no silver bullet, only the process that I have described within the pages of this book—the Profit Building Process.

Our results were remarkable, but it wasn't magic that improved our profit margin, just continuous evaluation and execution of cost-cutting measures for every line item on our P&L statement. We went form 26 to 52 EBITDA% (Earnings Before Interest Tax Depreciation and Amortization). We kept attacking our expenses, line by line.

This chapter includes a list of ideas for the additional line items that fall outside of salaries and personnel costs. These items have been used to create effective action plans in a variety of industries. You may be surprised at some of the options available, many of the costs we take for granted can often be reduced.

Like the list in chapter nine, this list can be used in a number of ways. The ideas offered here can be directly applied to your business, modified to suit your needs, or serve to jump-start your team's brainstorming sessions. These ideas are examples of the many creative solutions you can come to expect from your own PBT. Before using them, make sure they are appropriate for your business.

Category	*Idea Number*
Communications	51–56
Utilities	57–61
Professional Fees	62–79
Marketing	80–83
Public Relations	84–89
Insurance	90–92
Travel and Entertainment	93–97
Equipment Rental and Maintenance	98–100
Facilities Cost	101–104
Vehicles	105–107
Other Supplies and Services	108–112
Other Expenses	113–117
Lay Off Some Employees (as a last resort)	118

■ Communications

Snapshot

This category typically contains charges associated with (a) long-distance telephone, (b) cellular phone, (c) pagers, (d) T1 lines, (e) frame relay, (f) data lines, (g) fax lines, and so on.

Cost-Saving Ideas

51. Authorize a telecommunications consultant to analyze all of your communications costs in terms of rates charged, equipment used, programs offered, promotions available, T1 usage, cellular phone options, best pager scenario, long-distance carrier performance and

pricing, voice, fax and security line combinations, past bills, frame relay options, and so on. Structure the contract so that the consultant bills on the basis of percentage of costs saved or refunds received. In this way, there will be no cost to you if the consultant is not successful in improving your bottom line.

Comment: Review all areas of communication to ferret out those "pockets of expense" that often go unnoticed. Pagers and cell phones are usually ordered and distributed without the benefit of an organized plan. There are real and meaningful discounts if you shop around.

52. Continue to renegotiate rates and terms with the vendors who provide services.

Comment: Set up an ongoing procedure for constantly renegotiating rates and terms.

53. Contact your long-distance carrier to determine whether your company qualifies for the "best" long-distance rate on the basis of usage (time on line). This rate should be based on all of your locations, nationally and internationally, and the total usage should be considered in determining your "best" rate. The "best" rate is sometimes referred to as a software defined network (SDN).

Comment: When negotiating with your long-distance carrier, be sure to include all your organizations and/or businesses. You can negotiate better pricing when you present substantial total usage.

54. Once you qualify for a software defined network (SDN), you can aggregate other businesses that do not qualify for their own SDN onto yours and charge them a price that offers them a substantial discount on their long-distance cost and pays your company a premium per minute for the service.

Comment: If you have a network of members, vendors, customers, or strategic alliance partners who could be packaged together in a proposal to a long distance carrier, you will get the carrier's attention and, often, a better price. Assuming

*that your organization would qualify for the best price,
you can aggregate other associated organizations onto your
rate and negotiate with them a lower rate than they would
receive on their own.*

55. By offering your SDN area and services to your vendors, you are saving them real dollars. Use this leverage to receive better pricing on the product and/or services that these vendors are providing. You would also expect these vendors not to quote you standard price increases.

    Comment: You would now have an additional bit of leverage.

56. Measure your communications cost on the basis of a cost-per-unit test (guest check, widget, or the like) in order to determine locations for exerting additional control.

■ Utilities

Snapshot

This category typically contains charges associated with (a) gas and electricity usage, (b) HVAC usage, and so on.

Cost-Saving Ideas

57. Authorize a utility consultant to analyze your utility costs. Such consultants must know how to deal effectively with the local public service companies in order to discover advantages or missed opportunities associated with gas and electric services. They should be fully authorized to check existing equipment and records. They should be experienced in developing an index trend analysis and creating demand graphs to spot situations where you may have been overcharged.

They would also represent your issues to the Public Utilities Commission. Also, it is important to determine whether your business is being charged on the basis of peak demand. Sometimes businesses achieve peak demand only during periods of equipment start-up, and yet the higher rate is applied throughout the entire day. Evaluate ways to reduce the period of high usage, and try starting equipment on rotation. This will lower the peak demand—and your monthly expense.

58. Pay your consultant on the basis of a percentage of the savings associated with his or her action steps. The typical rate is 25% to 30% of the demonstrated savings and refunds over a specific period of time. There should be no charge if savings are not demonstrated.

59. Take energy conservation action steps, including setting thermostats at 72°F. Automatic HVAC controls should be put into place to control temperature during off-hours.

60. Turn off lights in conference rooms, rest rooms, and offices when they are not in use.

61. Turn off all lights not related to security at the close of business.

■ Professional Fees

> ### Snapshot
>
> This category typically includes charges associated with professional sevices: (a) legal and human resource–related fees, (b) proposals (domestic and international), (c) fees for technical services, and (d) other professional fees.

Cost-Saving Ideas

62. Talk about fees. If your lawyer does not bring up the subject of fees, you should. Do not be shy. In their busi-

ness, lawyers are free to set their own fees. The best time to discuss fees is at the beginning of a new legal matter.

63. Reach an understanding about how you will be charged. By the hour: $50 to $250 an hour. Flat fee: You are charged the same amount regardless of how long the lawyer spends on the project. Contingent fee: this is a percentage (such as 33%) of the amount the lawyer is able to obtain for you in a negotiated settlement.

64. Seek the most favorable arrangement for each case.

65. Try to settle cases rather than litigate.

66. Have lawyers design a form you can use in routine transactions.

67. Guarantee a minimum number of hours of work during the year.

68. Use less expensive lawyers for small collections or transactions.

    Comment: You may be surprised by some of the assignments given to outside attorneys. Pull your assignments over the last term. Are there items that could have been handled by less expensive attorneys?

69. Try to share costs when appropriate, and make sure there are no conflicts of interest.

70. Give the lawyer all appropriate records at the first meeting in order to avoid unnecessary phone calls regarding missing items. Do not add to the expense.

71. Insist on an itemized statement each month.

    Comment: Spend the time necessary to review these statements. Call and challenge the items you question—and don't get caught paying for the calls you make to challenge the items.

72. Suggest PBP approaches to the lawyer. Maybe you can save the lawyer some expenses that would offset or reduce your cost for the service.

Comment: Legal firms also need to reduce cost. Talk to them about setting up a PBT in exchange for a discount in your rate. This would be a true "win–win."

73. Keep abreast of legal developments in your field. Provide your lawyer with information about recent cases affecting your industry. This could reduce research costs.

74. See your lawyer during normal business hours.

75. Do not pay for travel time.

Comment: Review your itemized statements!

76. Consider adding a "house counsel."

Comment: Do the analysis. You may determine that a house counsel would save expenses.

77. Handle some items yourself.

Comment: There are some items that human resources could handle with a little guidance from counsel. Employment hearings and certain worker's compensation issues are examples.

78. Shop around but do not "lawyer-hop."

79. Attempt to negotiate rates on a regular basis.

■ Marketing

Snapshot
This category typically contains expenses associated with (a) advertising, (b) promotion, and (c) marketing.

Cost-Saving Ideas

80. Make sure advertising agencies do a post-buy analysis on all ad buys to determine whether target rates are achieved. Credits should be obtained if rating levels

have not been achieved. This would help stretch advertising dollars.

81. Seek syndication scenarios wherein a partner agrees to fund the development of commercials and campaigns for a percentage of revenues. This approach could save ad dollars and minimize the risk of advertising.

82. Advertising agencies should have more "skin in the game." Seek those that would partner on the basis of a percentage of revenue.

83. Publish a magazine using a desktop consultant, and distribute it to your customer base. Sell advertising space and commissionable products. Use the magazine to market your business.

    Comment: Depending on your customer base, this could be a big win for your organization!

■ Public Relations

Snapshot
This category typically contains communication costs associated with public relations.

Cost-Saving Ideas

84. If your business uses brochures to educate the public, consolidate and thereby reduce the number released annually.

85. Press Releases

    Reduce the dollars you pay PR agencies to write press releases and company backgrounders. Try having someone in your organization write the first draft of the story and give it to the agency to fine-tune, or hire a freelance writer to get local messages circulated. You will save lots of time and cost.

86. Free PR
    a. Create opportunities to cross-promote your business with your vendors, suppliers, and strategic partners.
    b. Stretch the impact of being a good corporate citizen. When you make a tax-deductible donation to local schools and charities (be sure to ask your employees for recommendations), include a press release. The school or charity will be happy to pass this along to editors.

87. Agency Performance Standards

    Plan how you want to get your message "in ink" and measure the agency's success rate against your plan. Adjust fees accordingly.

88. Create events out of everyday occurrences. Get them into print.

89. Instead of exhibiting at marginally successful trade shows, co-host a hospitality room or coffee break.

■ Insurance

Snapshot

This category typically contains charges associated with insurance (auto, umbrella, flood, crime, fiduciary, etc.).

Cost-Saving Ideas

90. Become familiar with all of your insurance policies—know which items are covered. Companies spend many dollars on damage claims, equipment replacement, and lawsuits without checking whether particular items are covered by insurance.

91. Constantly challenge third-party providers to reduce your insurance administration cost.

    Comment: If you want to see an area of potential cost savings, sit through a third-party provider review.

92. Determine at what point your administration department would save dollars by administering your insurance programs.

    Comment: There may be situations where it is more cost effective for the company to handle the administration.

■ Travel and Entertainment

> ### Snapshot
>
> This category typically contains charges associated with (a) airfare, (b) lodging, (c) entertainment, (d) car rentals, (e) parking, (f) tolls, (g) limousines, (h) taxis, and so on.

Cost-Saving Ideas

93. Determine whether your business should have an individual certified as an independent travel agent in order to receive discounts on hotel rooms, car rentals, and the like.

94. Determine whether your company should buy or lease an apartment or house for traveling employees rather than paying hotel rates.

95. Set up a policy that pays traveling employees a set per diem rate for meals and hotel rooms. This rate should be 20% less than the average of actual costs for the previous year. Employees should be paid this per diem regardless of whether they room in a more expensive or a less expensive hotel. You will notice a rapid reduction in travel costs, because employees will look for lower-cost rooms and meals in order to pocket dollars beneath the per diem rate. Consequently, the organization will realize a 20% reduction in hotel and meal costs.

96. Evaluate the feasibility of videoconferencing solutions to reduce travel costs.

    Comment: If your organization has substantial travel expenses, consult an expert in videoconferencing. Again, you will be surprised at the potential savings!

97. Institute a policy whereby all travel must be approved in advance and travel authorization forms must accompany expense reports. Institute a "no travel in December" policy. Most businesses experience a lower level of activity during this period because of the holidays.

■ Equipment Rental and Maintenance

Snapshot

This category typically includes charges associated with equipment rental and maintenance.

Cost-Saving Ideas

98. Lower your computer maintenance costs, and improve response time by using companies that specialize in shipping a replacement unit (such as a printer, terminal, or keyboard) to your designated location overnight prior to receipt of your defective unit. Your defective unit is then repaired and refurbished. Image Technology Solutions, Inc., located in Wood Dale, Illinois, is such a company. It ships replacement equipment and refurbishes your equipment while offering on-line ordering, warehousing, monthly reports, inventory control, and so on.

99. Regularly evaluate your current equipment maintenance provider. Compare that provider's services to your actual maintenance needs—the service may not be worth the monthly charge.

100. Continue to negotiate, negotiate, negotiate.

    Comment: You have real leverage here. Equipment suppliers make big profits in the out years. Front-end negotiations are the key.

■ Facilities Cost

Snapshot

This category typically contains charges related to your facilities: (a) building rent, (b) real property tax, (c) building maintenance, and so on.

Cost-Saving Ideas

101. Annually perform a property tax assessment comparing cost to build with fair market value.

102. Conduct a total cost of facility ownership (TCO) analysis to determine building cost stability, the potential for major systems replacements over time, and the often-overlooked workspace use changes that typically take place every 2–7 years. This type of analysis is beneficial for mobilizing your workforce for increased productivity.

    Comment: FIS Inc. (Facility Information Systems) located in Camarillo, California, provides TCO analysis and other software solutions that extend beyond traditional areas of facility management.

103. Evaluate whether excess property could be sold or leased in order to reduce carrying cost.

    Comment: Excess-property reviews always identify potential savings.

104. Evaluate whether a sell/lease-back program would have an expense/cost benefit to the organization.

■ Vehicles

Snapshot

This category typically includes charges associated with (a) vehicle leasing, (b) gasoline, (c) oil, (d) tires, (e) license fees, and so on.

Cost-Saving Ideas

105. If possible, purchase regular gasoline instead of premium.

      Comment: If you think this is a small issue, do an analysis on the last six months of gasoline expenses. You will probably find that your employees are purchasing only premium gas!

106. Install a gasoline credit card system that tracks mileage, records type of gas purchased, and confirms vehicles.

      Comment: This system will give you a new level of control, and you will realize big savings.

107. Consider or evaluate your company's policy for a car allowance vs. a company-car program.

■ Other Supplies and Services

Snapshot

This category typically includes charges associated with (a) reproduction, (b) office supplies, (c) armored cars, (d) uniforms, (e) freight, (f) coffee, and so on.

Cost-Saving Ideas

108. Evaluate your armored-car service to determine whether your number of pickups can be reduced, and whether managers can make the deposits.

109. Constantly negotiate and renegotiate with vendors. Seek price reductions or, at the least, no price increases.

110. Explore your ability to purchase goods and services at prices enjoyed by the largest corporations by evaluating e-business procurement solutions. Companies can receive incremental savings of 10%–20% net of fees on

items such as office supplies, temporary staffing, express mail, software, and travel services. These savings would be realized via a member-based purchasing consortium of indirect goods and services.

111. Make sure your business manages its trash. Recycle paper, reduce the number of trash bin pickups, and, if your business has "clean" trash, request larger bins. Make sure you are on the most economical program for your company.

112. Evaluate uniform programs. Are uniforms needed? Should employees pick up some of the cost? Should employees pay for cleaning? Do employees who have been terminated return uniforms? Are paychecks withheld until uniforms are returned? The laws on this vary from state to state, so check to see what is appropriate for your business.

■ Other Expenses

Snapshot

This category typically includes (a) bank charges, (b) donations, (c) cash over/short fees, (d) contributions, and so on.

Cost-Saving Ideas

113. Evaluate the charges that banks are assessing your organization. These fees are now very competitive, and banks will negotiate.

114. Evaluate whether electronic funds transfer can reduce costs for your business.

115. Make all your contributions to one not-for-profit organization. This reduces the cost of contributing to multiple organizations.

116. Determine whether your business would qualify for special tax incentives offered to businesses that expand or locate to state enterprise zones.

     Comment: This idea is related to labor savings such as the TJTC (targeted jobs tax credit).

117. Determine whether your business would qualify for any of the following tax credits.
     a. Investment tax credit for businesses located in enterprise zones.
     b. New business facility jobs credit that is available for new or expanded business facilities located in an enterprise zone that creates new jobs, adds value to agricultural products, and/or provides health insurance to employees.
     c. State sales and use tax exemptions for manufacturing and mining equipment used in an enterprise zone.
     d. Research and development tax credit for research and development carried on in an enterprise zone.
     e. Tax credits for private contributions to enterprise zone administrators.
     f. Tax credit for the rehabilitation of vacant commercial buildings located in an enterprise zone.

     Comment: Additional tax credits are not specific to salaries.

118.

> ### Lay off some employees
>
> *Comment: This should be your last resort!*

11 | How and Where to Get Started

What we call the beginning is often the end.
And to make an end is to make a beginning.
The end is where we start from.
—T. S. ELIOT

Congratulations! You now have a new perspective on what I believe will be the next wave to sweep over the business world. But unlike the many passing management fads we have seen come and go in the last decade, Profit Building is here to stay. It is the vital piece that has been missing from organizational design—a continuous process for profit improvement and cost reduction that should be a part of every business.

Now that you have finished reading the chapters on Profit Building, you are ready to begin. You are about to find out just how quickly one person can start to make a difference in an organization. The beauty of the PBP is that it can be applied to any organization, large or small. International organizations, large corporations, small businesses, individual departments, and franchises are all awaiting its arrival. Getting the process started will be an easy sell. The most difficult part will be overcoming the organization's resistance to this new approach.

As the saying goes, "there are few guarantees in life," but the following approach is certain to yield positive feedback from your supervisor, manager, vice president, business owner, president, CEO, board of directors or shareholders:

> No matter what position you hold in the organization, set up a meeting with your boss and tell him or her that you would like to put together a Profit Building Team made up of 5–8 employees from various departments within the organization.

Mention that the objective of this team is to use the Profit Building Process to generate a list of creative ideas that, when implemented, will start to generate cost reduction or profit improvement.

I guarantee that your boss will think for a fraction of a second and then say something like "What did you have in mind?" Or "How would you accomplish this?" Or "What can I do to help?" Or even "When can we get started?"

In order to prepare yourself, do a little homework on what help you will need from your boss or other employees in the organization. You may need a memorandum kicking off the process, authorization to provide training in Profit Building, time to use the Organizational Complexity Predictor, and so on. Once you have the attention and support of your boss, you are ready to begin. Here are several suggestions for getting started:

1. Use this book as a step-by-step guide, beginning with Chapter 1.
2. Meet with senior management from other departments to determine who would be good candidates for the PBT.
3. Pick your team and have them read *Profit Building*. Have your team members help implement the process.
4. Seek help from your training department in training the team and preparing the organization.
5. Introduce a company-wide reading program in which each employee reads *Profit Building*. Many will volunteer to be members of the PBT.

6. Hold a seminar on Profit Building and ask for volunteers for the PBT.

7. Bring in a consultant as an outsider to help take your organization through the PBP.

8. Seek recommendations from human resources on key employees who would make good members for the PBT.

9. Hold a company-wide contest for cost reduction or profit improvement ideas. The winning suggestions can be the ticket for entry to the PBT.

10. Have a company-wide drawing of names.

Do whatever works for your organization. The point is to get started.

Remember: *Prepare the team and the organization to handle the changes to come.* That should get you over the initial resistance that any new program encounters. Once the Profit Building Process gets started, you will discover endless avenues for cost reduction and profit improvement that you probably never considered before. Let *Profit Building* serve as your road map—the rest is up to you and your organization.

I have enjoyed writing this book. It is my hope that it will be of as much benefit to you and your organization as its concepts have been to me and the companies where I have applied them.

Good Luck!

Appendix
Profit Building
Process Forms

Following are blank forms designed to help you implement the PBP. Copies of the enclosed Organizational Complexity Predictor (described in Chapter 5), should be distributed to all employees. Questions Brainstorming (Form A), Taking Action and Documenting (Form B), and Reviewing and Following Up (Form C) are for the PBT. They are meant to help you and your team organize and prioritize the questions that are generated and help track the progress of proposed innovations and changes.

Organizational Complexity Predictor

This questionnaire is used to predict the level of difficulty that an organization would have when attempting to manage innovation or change.

Questions	Rating (X)
1. In the organization, is there a continuous need for various departments to work together in order for a product or service to be delivered?	Low 1 2 3 4 5 6 7 8 9 10 High ☐☐☐☐☐☐☐☐☐☐
2. Is the organization strategic in its action(s)?	Low 1 2 3 4 5 6 7 8 9 10 High ☐☐☐☐☐☐☐☐☐☐
3. Is there frequent turnover in middle and upper management?	Low 1 2 3 4 5 6 7 8 9 10 High ☐☐☐☐☐☐☐☐☐☐
4. Is there frequent turnover in the lower levels of the organization?	Low 1 2 3 4 5 6 7 8 9 10 High ☐☐☐☐☐☐☐☐☐☐
5. Are new ideas quickly adopted and diffused throughout the organization?	Low 1 2 3 4 5 6 7 8 9 10 High ☐☐☐☐☐☐☐☐☐☐
6. Is the generation of new ideas encouraged in the organization?	Low 1 2 3 4 5 6 7 8 9 10 High ☐☐☐☐☐☐☐☐☐☐
7. Does the organization have resources set aside to reward the generation of new ideas?	Low 1 2 3 4 5 6 7 8 9 10 High ☐☐☐☐☐☐☐☐☐☐

8. Does the organization communicate a wish to generate new ideas from its employees?	Low 1 2 3 4 5 6 7 8 9 10 High ☐☐☐☐☐☐☐☐☐☐
9. Are new procedures easily rolled out and implemented in the organization?	Low 1 2 3 4 5 6 7 8 9 10 High ☐☐☐☐☐☐☐☐☐☐
10. Does the organization use project planning when it undertakes a major project?	Low 1 2 3 4 5 6 7 8 9 10 High ☐☐☐☐☐☐☐☐☐☐
11. Are "end users" of new procedures given the opportunity to provide input before the development of these new procedures?	Low 1 2 3 4 5 6 7 8 9 10 High ☐☐☐☐☐☐☐☐☐☐
12. Are "end users" given the opportunity to modify or reinvent existing procedures?	Low 1 2 3 4 5 6 7 8 9 10 High ☐☐☐☐☐☐☐☐☐☐
13. Is top management committed to change and innovation?	Low 1 2 3 4 5 6 7 8 9 10 High ☐☐☐☐☐☐☐☐☐☐
14. Does the organization learn from its mistakes?	Low 1 2 3 4 5 6 7 8 9 10 High ☐☐☐☐☐☐☐☐☐☐
15. Is senior management hired from within the organization?	Low 1 2 3 4 5 6 7 8 9 10 High ☐☐☐☐☐☐☐☐☐☐

16. Does senior management solicit new ideas from within the organization?	Low 1 2 3 4 5 6 7 8 9 10 High ☐ ☐ ☐ ☐ ☐ ☐ ☐ ☐ ☐ ☐
17. Are there innovation champions within the ranks of senior management?	Low 1 2 3 4 5 6 7 8 9 10 High ☐ ☐ ☐ ☐ ☐ ☐ ☐ ☐ ☐ ☐
18. Does the organization have an aggressive e-strategy for planning e-commerce and e-tactics?	Low 1 2 3 4 5 6 7 8 9 10 High ☐ ☐ ☐ ☐ ☐ ☐ ☐ ☐ ☐ ☐
19. Does the organization give cash incentives for new ideas?	Low 1 2 3 4 5 6 7 8 9 10 High ☐ ☐ ☐ ☐ ☐ ☐ ☐ ☐ ☐ ☐
20. Does the organization have an aggressive program for attracting female and minority employees and vendors?	Low 1 2 3 4 5 6 7 8 9 10 High ☐ ☐ ☐ ☐ ☐ ☐ ☐ ☐ ☐ ☐

Overall Rating

Please average the ratings for all of the above questions to obtain an overall rating.	Low 1 2 3 4 5 6 7 8 9 10 High ☐ ☐ ☐ ☐ ☐ ☐ ☐ ☐ ☐ ☐

The following is used only by the manager performing the evaluation.

If your organization's overall rating is	Then:
8, 9, or 10	The environment of the organization is *adaptable to change.* The organization should receive change or new innovation very well.
5, 6, or 7	The environment of the organization is *moderate in receptiveness* to the adoption/diffusion of *change* and innovation.
2, 3, or 4	The environment of the organization is *resistant to change.* Characteristics include employee dissatisfaction, frequent setbacks, and low levels of innovation receptiveness. Concentrated actions are required in order to manage change throughout the organization.
1	This organization *will not adopt or diffuse a change* or innovation. Replace management and start over.

Form A—Example

Questions—PBP

Date: _____

Team: _____

Rank	Questions
1.	
2.	
3.	
4.	
5.	
6.	
7.	
8.	
9.	
10.	
11.	
12.	

Form B—Example

Taking Action and Documenting – PBP

PBP Question	Action Steps	Person(s) Responsible	Target Date	Measure-ment	Contingency Plan	Review and Follow-up	Next PBP Question
PBP Question	Action Steps	Person(s) Responsible	Target Date	Measure-ment	Contingency Plan	Review and Follow-up	Next PBP Question

Form C—Example

Reviewing and Following Up—PBP

PBP Question	Situation Analysis	Profitability Improvement
1.		
2.		
3.		
4.		
5.		
6.		
7.		
8.		
9.		

Footnotes

Chapter 2

1. Wally Wood, "Can Telcos Survive?" *Internet Telephony*, March 4, 1996.

2. Alex Markels and Matt Murray, "Call It Dumbsizing: Why Some Companies Regret Cost-Cutting," *Wall Street Journal*, May 15, 1996.

3. Ibid.

4. Ibid.

5. Nathan Seppa, "Downsizing: A New Form of Abandonment," *APA Monitor*, May 1996. Quoted from an interview with Steve Kozlowski, Ph.D.

Chapter 4

1. Roger Von Oech, *A Whack on the Side of the Head* (New York: Warner Books, 1990) p. 14.

2. Peter Drucker, *Managing the Future: The 1990's and Beyond* (New York: Penguin Books, 1992) p. 298.

3. Paul Hersey and Kenneth H. Blanchard, *Management of Organizational Behavior* (Englewood Cliffs, NJ: Prentice-Hall, 1993), p. 176.

Chapter 5

1. Paul Hersey and Kenneth H. Blanchard, *Management of Organizational Behavior* (Englewood Cliffs, NJ: Prentice-Hall, 1993), pp. 373–374.
2. Ron Zemke with Dick Schaaf, *The Service Edge: 101 Companies That Profit from Customer Care* (New York: Penguin Books, 1990) p. 29.
3. Geoffrey Bellman, *Your Signature Path* (San Francisco: Berrett-Koehler Publishers, 1996), p. 102.

Chapter 7

1. H. James Harrington, *The Improvement Process* (New York: McGraw-Hill, 1987), p. 152.

Chapter 8

1. Robert Fritz, *Corporate Tides: The Inescapable Laws of Organizational Structure* (San Francisco: Berrett-Koehler Publishers, 1996), p. 127.
2. Alan Webber, interview with Peter Senge, "Learning for a Change," *Fast Company*, May, 1999, p. 186.

Bibliography

BELLMAN, GEOFFREY. Your Signature Path. San Francisco: Berrett-Koehler Publishers, 1996.

DRUCKER, PETER. *Managing the Future: The 1990's and Beyond.* New York: Penguin Books, 1992.

FRITZ, ROBERT. *Corporate Tides: The Inescapable Laws of Organizational Structure.* San Francisco: Berrett-Koehler Publishers, 1996.

HARRINGTON, H. JAMES. *The Improvement Process.* New York: McGraw-Hill, 1987.

HERSEY, PAUL, and KENNETH H. BLANCHARD. *Management of Organizational Behavior.* Englewood Cliffs, NJ: Prentice-Hall, 1993.

HUBER, GEORGE P., and WILLIAM H. GLICK. *Organizational Change and Redesign: Ideas and Insights for Improving Performance.* New York: Oxford University Press, 1995.

MARKELS, ALEX, AND MATT MURRAY. "Call it Dumbsizing: Why Some Companies Regret Cost-Cutting." *Wall Street Journal,* May 15, 1996.

SEPPA, NATHAN. "Downsizing: A New Form of Abandonment." *APA Monitor,* May 1996.

VON OECH, ROGER. *A Whack on the Side of the Head.* New York: Warner Books, 1990.

WEBBER, ALAN. "Learning for a Change." *Fast Company,* May 1999.

WOOD, WALLY. "Can Telcos Survive?" *Telephony Magazine,* March 4, 1996.

ZEMKE, RON. *The Service Edge: 101 Companies That Profit from Customer Care.* New York: Penguin Books, 1990.

About the Author

Perry J. Ludy is a senior executive with more than 25 years experience with leading corporations and entrepreneurial companies. His consulting firm, LUDYCO, International specializes in helping domestic and international organizations develop creative approaches to building profits and managing innovation. Ludy also speaks, conducts seminars, provides corporate training, and consults on mergers and acquisitions. He has worked for leading US companies including PepsiCo, Inc., Procter & Gamble, and Imperial Corporation of America.

Additional Resources
For **PROFIT BUILDING**

- **Training Materials and Merchandise**

- **Video**

- **Seminars**

- **Keynote Speeches**

- **Workshops**

- **Consulting Services**

- **Promotional Materials**

please contact:

LUDYCO International
1440 Whalley Avenue #228
New Haven, CT 06515-1100

203-393-7210 phone
203-393-7214 fax
ludyco@mindspring.com
www.perryludy.com

Index